FLOORS

Thomas Lane

conran
OCTOPUS

First published in 1996 b
Conran Octopus Limite
37 Shelton Street
London
WC2H 9HN

This edition first published 1998

Commissioning Editor: Denny Hemming

Senior Editor: Catriona Woodburn
Art Editor: Tony Seddon
Picture Researcher: Rachel Davies
Production Controller: Mano Mylvaganam

Designers: Isabel de Cordova, Amanda Lerwill
Artwork Visualizer: Jean Morley
Illustrator: Clare Melinsky

A catalogue record for this book is available from the British Library.

ISBN 1 85029 977 3

Printed in China

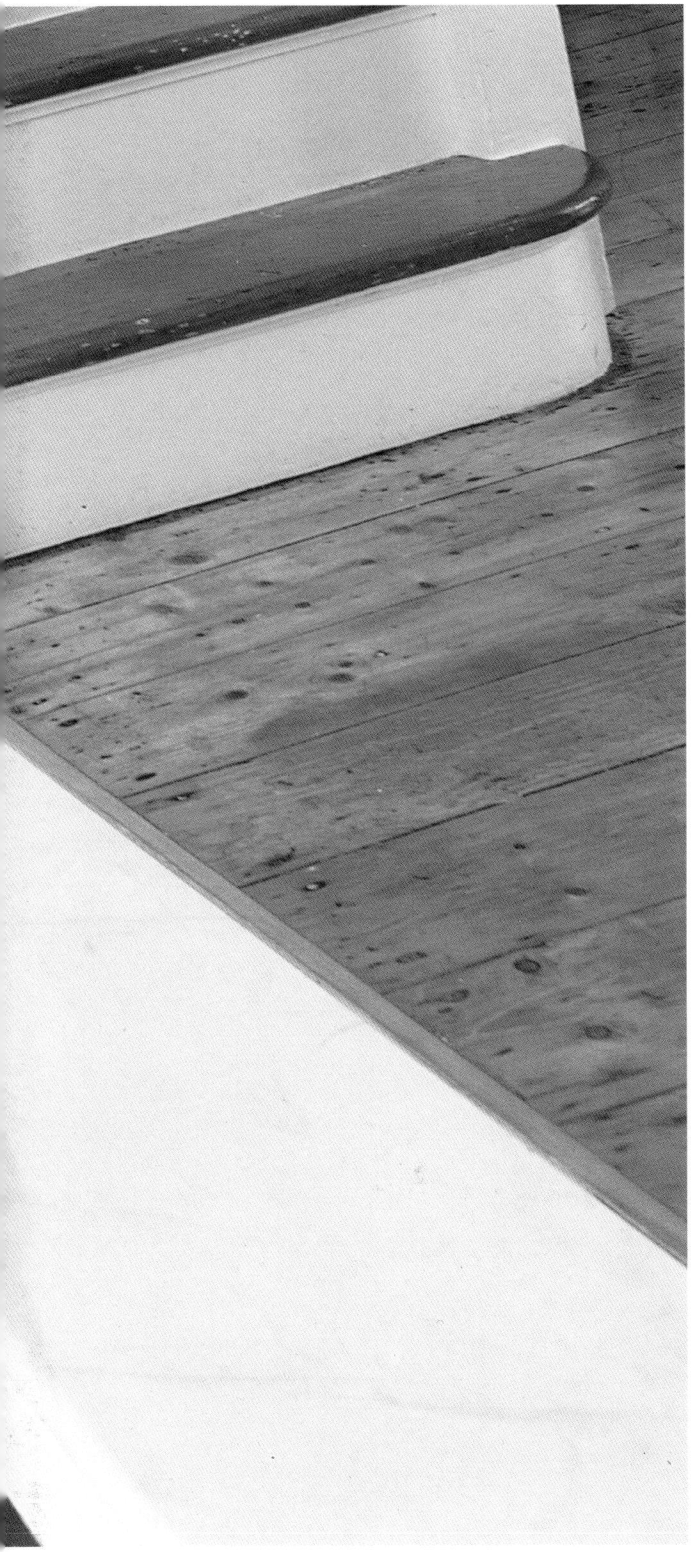

CONTENTS

Getting started

Whatever its condition, provided your floor is structurally sound it can be restored or covered using one of the many options available to the home decorator. An older home may have wooden floors that can be sanded and varnished to give a fine finish, and even a concrete floor can be painted to stunning effect. Rugs, floor tiles and vinyl can be found to suit every taste, while natural floor-coverings, such as rush matting, combine the beauty of a wood floor with the softness of a carpet.

▲ *Cool concrete painted a royal blue picks up on the fresh tone of the chairs in the kitchen and contrasts with the warm tones of the pale wood in the foreground. The neat demarcation between the two different materials allows the worker in the office in the foreground to separate work from the comforts of the living area beyond.*

Floors and floor-coverings are not indestructible and there comes a day when something has to be done about the threadbare carpet, the tatty vinyl or the filthy, cracked floorboards. Even if the flooring is still in fairly good condition, it may be that you have grown tired of it or, having moved into a new dwelling, you do not share the former occupant's taste. Yet other factors may be involved in the decision to change a floor-covering. Perhaps a dusty carpet that causes uncontrollable sneezing is harbouring a population of house-dust mites and a non-fabric floor-covering would be less allergenic. Maybe a wood floor is looking scratched or the colour is not quite right for a new decorative scheme. Although it may seem that the only solution is to rip up the lot and start again, this is not the only course of action open to you – nor is it necessarily desirable.

The first step when considering a new floor is to examine the options available and to decide whether they are affordable. Most decent-quality floor-coverings are expensive, although the cheaper-quality carpets and vinyls are among the most economical floor-coverings currently available. If you are restricted to a tight budget, consider renovating the existing floor (see pages 8–29). The result could look much better than a cheap carpet would and is one of the most potentially rewarding, if challenging, of flooring options.

Houses and some flats built before the 1960s will probably have floors constructed from pine boards, or even oak or parquet. Bald carpets and scruffy vinyl or linoleum may be past salvation but try lifting a corner to see what is underneath (see pages 8–9). People frequently cover up a very good wood floor with a carpet, and what you find could be the basis of a whole new and exciting range of possibilities.

Newer houses and flats and older dwellings that have been extensively modernized may have floors constructed from chipboard or concrete. Although these materials lack the charm of old floorboards they can be brightened up considerably with paint (see pages 20–27). Even concrete can be

▲ *This room has the original oak floorboards often found in much older houses. This type of floor tends to age gracefully and naturally, and looks good simply waxed and polished in any environment; here the floorboards perfectly complement an informal arrangement of pale furnishings that gives an uncluttered impression.*

painted to imitate a more expensive material such as limestone flooring and, of course, it will have the solidity associated with the real thing.

Indeed, there are very few existing floors that cannot be improved by one of the wide range of decorative treatments now available. For instance, floors that really seem past all hope but which are structurally sound can have plywood shapes fixed to them which are then painted or stained, perhaps in imitation of flagstones or marble tiles (see pages 26–27). Such a treatment can transform a rough old floor for very little outlay and will look far more sophisticated than cheap carpet.

Bare wood or concrete is not to everyone's taste; nor is either appropriate to every situation. Fortunately, it is a relatively easy matter to change their appearance completely by adding a new layer of floor-covering. Flooring materials are diverse and within each group there are variations and styles to suit every taste and requirement. All can be quick and easy to install. Hard tiles and stone provide hard-wearing flooring suitable for anywhere receiving a lot of foot traffic or where water is present (see pages 40–43). Flexible flooring such as vinyl or linoleum, in sheet or tile form, offers softer, waterproof options suitable for kitchens and utility areas, and, if cushioned, is especially kind to the feet (see pages 48–51). Even new wood floors can be laid without much effort or skill (see pages 58–61). And for total underfoot luxury there is today a huge range of carpets and natural floor-coverings – unsurpassed for variety and price range (see pages 64–67).

Varied as they are, all these exciting floor-coverings usually require a sound, level floor upon which to rest in order to ensure that they look good and wear well. Before laying any new flooring the existing floor should be checked for any faults and repaired or prepared as appropriate for the new flooring material (see pages 34–37).

With so many flooring options on offer, there is nothing to stop anyone from having beautiful floors, no matter what the size of their pocket. Free up your imagination and you will achieve surprisingly dramatic effects.

▲ Natural floor-coverings have become very popular recently due to the wide choice available and their relatively low cost; they also look good in almost any setting. The strong texture of the rush matting here lends relief to the flat features of this room and the neutral colour works well with the vivid colour scheme.

◄ Tiles are one of the most versatile flooring materials, being both almost indestructible and waterproof. The handmade ceramic tiles in this shower room give it a more countrified look, the hand-painted tiles on the floor and tiles cut into pyramids on the skirting adding visual interest to an otherwise tiny and plain space.

Decorating existing floors

Although an existing floor may appear beyond redemption, you do not necessarily have to cover it up with a new and expensive flooring material. As long as the floor is structurally sound, it can either be restored to its former glory or brightened up with a whole range of inspiring decorative improvements. If the floor is covered with an old flooring material, it is always worth peeling this back some way, and in at least two different places, to check the condition of the floor underneath.

Floorboards may look worn and dirty but it is surprising how good they can look when they have been sanded (see pages 16–17) and varnished. For renovation, though, they do need to be in reasonable condition; any damaged boards should be replaced and gaps filled (see pages 14–15). If the colour of the boards is not quite commensurate with the room's decoration, they can be painted or treated in any number of ways. A painted design can look breathtaking and will always be a talking point for visitors.

Cracks and pits in concrete floors can be repaired fairly easily (see pages 34–35) and then painted with a plain colour or any type of pattern imaginable. Alternatively, a concrete floor can be covered with a pattern of plywood squares which can be cunningly painted to imitate flagstones or a marble-tiled floor (see pages 26–27).

One of the few floor surfaces that cannot be easily changed with paint is tiles; the paint will chip off in the hard wear such a floor is likely to receive, especially in the places where tiles are usually laid, such as in kitchens and bathrooms. Unwanted floor tiles must either be physically removed or covered with another floor-covering, such as might be used for concrete. Another surface that does not accept paint is vinyl, because the paint reacts with the plastic and peels off.

Having made the decision to renovate an existing floor rather than to cover it up, the first step is to decide how the finished floor is to look, for this will determine what preparation the floor will need.

Varnished floors

One of the most popular ways of improving an existing floor, and one that can be done quickly and easily, is to machine-sand old floorboards and varnish them for protection (see pages 16–17, 28–29). The result can look particularly attractive if the boards are hardwood, such as oak or ash. It is more likely, however, that an existing floor will be constructed of pine or deal boards. These cheap softwoods were used extensively for flooring up to the 1960s, after which even cheaper materials manufactured from reclaimed wood became standard.

▲ *Sanded old floorboards are an economical and practical choice of flooring, considering how many older homes were built with perfectly serviceable wooden floors. This floor has simply been sanded and given several coats of gloss varnish for a rich, deep shine; bright light pouring through the windows bounces off it.*

One difficulty with old pine floors is that the wood darkens over the years, tending to become a fiery ginger colour. And as the protective varnish coat yellows with age, it exacerbates the hotness of this colour, which tends to clash with many colours commonly used in decorating. Cool blues and greens are perhaps the only colours that sit comfortably with sanded pine floorboards. Thankfully, however, it is an easy matter to alter the colour of pine boards to something more sympathetic to contemporary taste.

Stained floors

Stains (see pages 18–19) modify the colour of floorboards without affecting the appearance of the wood's natural grain. As they always darken the wood, only use stains in situations where this is not a problem. Dark-stained boards are an excellent backdrop ▷

▲ *Painted concrete is amazingly practical and hard-wearing; this bathroom has been painted with an abstract design that not only looks good but is also waterproof, cheap to implement and easily cleaned. The major investment to consider for a floor like this is your own time and patience – and creative skills.*

◀ *Paint is one of the cheapest and most versatile ways of transforming an old floor. This floor has been given a new lease of life with this colourful and boldly patterned floorcloth; originally painted on canvas in a studio it was then transported to this location and installed wall-to-wall. The overall impression is of a painted floor.*

for richly coloured rugs and carpets, although it is important to select a neutral colour rather than a strong one such as mahogany, which would clash with a rug that is predominantly red, for instance. Formal rooms – traditional drawing rooms, dining rooms and libraries – look more sophisticated and imposing with darker floors. As richer and darker colours tend to be used to decorate these rooms, which are often used at night with soft lighting, evoking a more intimate feel, darker floors are a more discreet choice. Of course, a darker floor can also work successfully with a very light room, either for dramatic effect or as a backdrop for darker rugs. And dark colours tend to appear less oppressive the lower down they are used in the room; a dark oak floor can work well with pale walls and furnishing.

Bleached floors

Wood darkens with age; sometimes this can turn the wood very dark, or an unattractive colour, where a lighter colour is more desirable for a more vital and contemporary look. Lightening the wood while retaining its 'woody' appearance can be difficult, as applying transparent colour will always darken it. Chemical bleaching is one solution to the problem.

Light floors are ideal for informal settings, such as kitchens and eating areas, or in any situation that calls for a fresh and airy atmosphere. Most furnishings will work well with light-coloured floors, as the floor fades against the predominant colours to provide a delicate backdrop. Darker pieces of furniture are accentuated against a light floor, useful for drawing attention to a particularly fine item.

Limed floors

Hardwood floors such as oak or ash can be lightened by using the traditional technique of liming (see pages 18–19). This lightens a whole area generally, but specifically lightens the actual grain of the wood resulting in a very graphic look. Liming is a labour-intensive business but the results are stunning. Staining the wood black, or indeed any other colour, before the liming process is started creates an even more exciting look by combining light and dark tones in a natural, free-form way that virtually becomes the focal point of a room.

▲ *Wood takes paint very well – both opaque paint and transparent colour that allows the grain of the wood to show through. This wooden floor has been painted with a very loose chequerboard pattern embellished with naive motifs to complement the kilims on the bed and to help create a tribal style.*

▶ *A wooden floor has been painted here with the same neutral, pale tones as the walls and ceiling. This approach tends to accentuate the colours of the features and furniture in the room, as the floor becomes part of an all-enveloping, unobtrusive backdrop, punctuated only by the strong lines of the beams and boards.*

Painted floors

Floors that are in poor condition or which are made from very plain materials such as concrete or chipboard can be transformed with conventional paint which will cover any number of blemishes and provide an evenly coloured surface. The floor can be painted any colour imaginable, from white for an ultra-light look to black for the ultimate light-absorbing surface. Neutral greys and beiges are perfect for non-controversial and flattering backgrounds to almost anything.

If plain colour seems a little dull, patterns – anything from simple squares to a painted imitation of an intricate Persian carpet – can be incorporated into a floor. Floors can be stencilled with any type of design (see pages 22–23) or covered with chequerboard squares (see pages 24–25). Even natural-stone looks can be effected to transform concrete or chipboard into a marble or flagstone floor (see pages 26–27).

Painting a floor is quick and cheap, and easily changed if it is not quite right or if you decide you are bored with it. Matching the floor colour to a fabric sample can be effective too, and nowadays, for a modest fee, some paint manufacturers offer a spectrophotometer service that exactly matches a paint colour with a supplied fabric sample.

Sealing

Once a surface has been sanded or stained it needs to be protected against general wear and tear with one of several wood finishes such as varnish or lacquer (see pages 28–29); how heavy-duty the protection needs to be will depend more on the situation of the floor, than on any inherent quality of the raw material.

◀ *If still structurally sound, pine floorboards typically found in Victorian houses are full of decorative potential. They have been transformed here by a subtle painted border that echoes the colour of the stairs while the rest of the floor has been left plain and simply sealed – a straightforward but effectively decorative treatment.*

Directory of decorative finishes

Wood floors can be finished in a number of ways. They can be left *au naturel*, with nothing added or taken away, or they can be coloured with stain or paint. In addition, dark wood can be lightened to counteract the effects of ageing or to highlight the grain. And unless a wood floor has been finished with a floor paint or liming wax, it will have to be protected with varnish or lacquer.

1

2

Opaque colour

Opaque colour is what most people think of as 'ordinary paint', which is used for painting walls and ceilings. It is ideal for painting unattractive flooring chipboard and is also useful for poor floorboards that have been repaired with lots of wood filler. Two to three coats will create a pure, unbroken colour that will completely disguise any flaws. Opaque paint is available in an almost infinite range of ready-mixed colours as well as in many finishes and types. It is perfect for very pale colours or if a plain look is desired but darker tones are strong and dominating, which may look heavy if the colour is not chosen with care. Most types of opaque paint can be used on floors but they will usually need the additional protection of a varnish. Oil-based eggshells and gloss paints used in light-traffic areas such as bedrooms may not require additional protection – nor proper floor paint. But water-based paints are the most user-friendly; they have no harmful fumes and brushes are easier to wash out. **1**

Stained floors

Wood stains or dyes are concentrated colours designed to penetrate the wood and effect a dramatic colour change without affecting the appearance of the wood's surface. They are normally associated with types of wood, the idea being that the application of the stain will transform an ordinary pine floor into something rather more exotic. The reality is that the colour of the wood influences the final colour: the lighter the stain, the greater will be the effect of the original colour of the wood. Stains are also available in quite bright colours, and colours of the same brand can be intermixed. Water-, spirit- or oil-based stains are all so fast drying that it can be difficult to obtain an even finish. Stains always need protecting with a varnish or lacquer.

Varnish stain is an alternative product that stains and protects the wood in one application, although it is unlikely to be sufficiently tough for areas of heavy wear. **2**

Transparent colour

Transparent colour is used to modify the colour of an existing surface, retaining its texture and character rather than obliterating it. It has a much gentler quality than opaque paint, enabling the use of vivid or dark hues without the result looking heavy and solid. Complex and interesting colours can be built up in several coats for a rich and glowing look that is unobtainable with opaque paints. To make up transparent colour, mix artist's colour into a transparent medium such as a water- or oil-based varnish to create almost any colour imaginable. The colour can be used over the whole floor area or to create a design, an easier task with transparent colour than opaque colour as only one coat is required. If woody colours are used the effect will resemble inlay or marquetry. The only possible disadvantage of using transparent colour is that the floor will always end up darker. **3**

Semi-transparent colour

Also known as semi-opaque colour, this is useful for situations where the aim is to preserve the grain of a wood floor, yet also lighten the colour of the floor. It is a mixture of transparent and opaque colour, usually made up by mixing white paint with a clear varnish. The white pigment in the paint partially covers the existing wood but not to such a degree that the grain of the wood is lost. The pigment has a lightening effect and colour can be added to change the colour of the wood slightly. The final result can look a little milky, depending on how much white is added, but the wood is still very visible. **4**

3

4

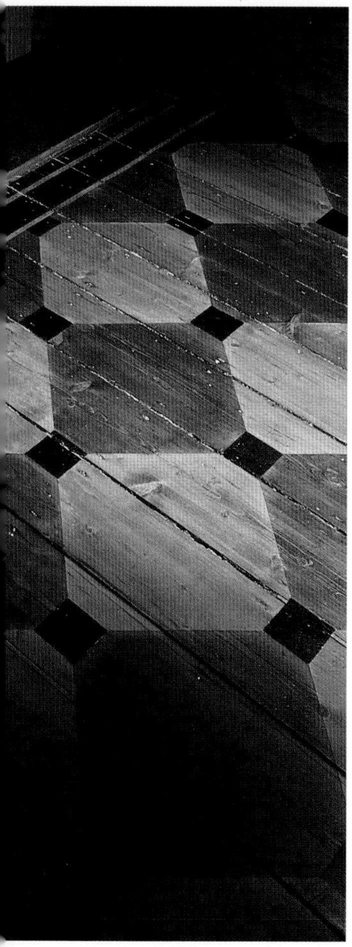

5

Bleached floors

Chemical bleaches are useful for lightening wood that has darkened with age, without affecting the appearance of the grain. The chemicals are applied to the bare wood and left to react and lighten the surface. When the wood reaches the desired colour, the chemicals are neutralized and the floor can be varnished.

Another way to lighten the colour of wood is to rub a little white paint into the grain, although this must be done sparingly to prevent the grain being completely obliterated. 5

Limed floors

Liming is a wood treatment that fills the grain of oak and ash, lightens the surface and gives the texture a very graphic appearance. Oak is particularly improved by liming. Traditionally, real lime was used but it is caustic and damages the skin and nails; more benign alternatives are now available, which have the same effect. They are applied and rubbed off when dry, leaving the grain white. To introduce brighter colours, stain the wood before liming it. But always protect the limed wood with a coat of varnish.

Liming wax

Liming wax is another product available for lightening wood. It is a white-pigmented wax that is simply rubbed into the grain and buffed with a cloth. Less messy to use than liming paste, it cannot be varnished as no varnish or paint product will adhere to wax. It is essential, then, to rewax the floor once the treatment wears off.

Varnished or lacquered floors

Varnish and lacquer seal plain wood floors with a protective finish. Different sealers change the colour and character of the wood to different degrees and some also change colour with age. Varnish, available in matt, satin or gloss finishes, is the most commonly used sealer. Both traditional oil-based and acrylic varnishes are suitable. They are widely available and easy to apply, whereas hard-wearing floor lacquers usually require more care and entail more work. As a rule solvent-based products bring out the natural colour of the wood better, giving it a richness and depth unmatched by water-based varieties; of the two, however, solvent-based sealers are the less user-friendly.

Repairing and preparing floorboards

▶ *These old floorboards are typical of what you are likely to find under an old carpet. Although the boards can sometimes look worryingly uneven and worn, modern sanding machines cut quickly through the wood to provide a smooth and level surface – ready for painting and sealing.*

Estimating quantities

There is nothing more irritating than running out of something halfway through a job and having to stop work to buy extra supplies. Before you start a renovation or decorating job, take time to assess accurately how much of which materials you will need. It is always worth buying a little extra to compensate for mistakes and wastage. Remember to check too on whether you have the correct tools and enough nails.

Replacement floorboards

Although floorboards are usually 18mm (¾in) thick, check the thickness as well as the width of your boards before ordering replacements and specify these dimensions as 'planed all round' (PAR) to the supplier. When calculating the length of timber required, bear in mind that each replacement board must run from joist to joist; the nails holding the boards down indicate the position of the joists. If a large quantity of wood is needed remember that new boards are about 4m (13ft) long, and offcuts may well be too short for practical use. Over-order by about 10 per cent to be safe.

Sandpaper for sanding machine

Estimating how much sandpaper you will need to sand a room is not critical, as the shops that hire out sanding machinery will also supply the paper on a sale-or-return basis. You will need more of the coarsest grade than of the finer grades; five sheets of grit 24, and two each of grit 40, grit 80 and grit 100 should be sufficient to sand 30 sq m (36 sq yd) of pine floorboards in reasonable condition.

Paint and stain

It is difficult to be precise about paint requirements, but you will require 2–2.5 litres (about ½ gallon) for each base coat for a 30 sq m (36 sq yd) floor.

It is difficult to estimate how much wood stain would be needed to cover the same area as much depends on the type of stain and the porosity of the wood. As a rough guide, however, 1 litre (⅕ gallon) should cover approx. 10–20 sq m (12–24 sq yd).

Varnish and floor lacquer

To seal a 30 sq m (36 sq yd) floor area you will need approx. 2 litres (½ gallon) of oil- or water-based varnish per coat. Floor lacquer does not spread quite as far: 3 litres (⅔ gallon) will be required per coat.

Preparing a wood floor for painting or sealing

Any floor that is going to look good needs to have any defects corrected at an early stage. Damage must be repaired before a floor can be sanded or painted. Old floorboards can sometimes crack along their length and any damaged boards will have to be replaced. Floorboards can also shrink with age, leaving unsightly gaps. The best and easiest way to deal with gaps between floorboards is to try to live with them; they are part of the charm of an old floor, and on a painted floor the eye tends to focus on the lines of a design rather than on the gaps. But this is not always practical and you will probably have to fill them.

Before sealing, the floor will probably need sanding, a process which removes the top few millimetres of the wood to leave a fresh, clean, ready-to-finish surface. It is not always necessary to sand a floor before painting it, however. A good dirt-removing scrub may suffice, but where old wax or paint needs to be removed, white spirit, paint stripper and lots of work will be required.

Lifting and replacing floorboards

Lifting square-edged boards is comparatively easy. Use a bolster chisel to lever up the board at its end, taking care not to damage the adjacent board. Once it is clear of the surface, support it in this position with a piece of wood and lever the board up with the bolster chisel where it is nailed to the joist. Do not try to lift the board up from the end as it will almost certainly break in half. Repeat this procedure until the damaged area has been lifted; moving to the middle of the nearest joist, support the board and scribe a line across the board – using a try square to ensure the cut is square. Cut the board with a cross-cut saw (see pages 36–37), taking care not to damage adjacent boards. Measure a new board and cut it to fit the removed section. Nail it in place with lost-head nails.

Repairing wooden floors

1 *Lift a damaged board by using a bolster chisel as a lever, and then support it with an offcut of wood.*

Replacing a tongued-and-grooved board is more difficult as all the boards interlock. You will have to cut the tongue off the board to be lifted before levering it up. The easiest way to do this is to cut along the edge of the board using a circular saw (see pages 36–37); to avoid cutting through pipes and cables, set the blade to cut at a depth of 18mm (¾in). You can use a sharp chisel and mallet to start the cut and then continue with a handsaw, returning to the chisel when you reach a joist, but it is much more awkward. Either way, fill the hole with a square-edged board.

Filling gaps

Small gaps can be filled with papier-mâché. Larger gaps that reach from joist to joist should be disguised with a wooden fillet. Measure the gap, cut a corresponding width off the edge of a spare board and glue it in position with wood glue.

If the whole floor is full of gaps it will probably be easier and more satisfactory to lift all the boards, push them tightly together and re-secure them. Number the boards as you lift them so that you replace them in the same order. You will end up with a large gap: fill it with a new board or part of one.

Dealing with nail heads

Remove any old staples and carpet tacks and hammer down any proud nail heads. If you are machine-sanding the floor, you do not have to punch them below the surface, but to save on sanding pads it is sensible.

▲ *It is worth noting that sanding and sealing stairs is a particularly time-consuming and awkward task. Sometimes it is not only easier to leave old floors in their natural state, it is also more authentic. This staircase is made from old pine that helps to evoke a sense of rustic simplicity which is wholly in keeping with the decoration of the rest of the house.*

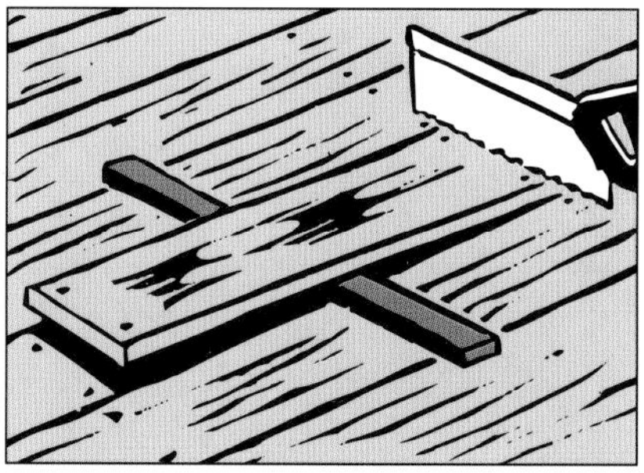

2 *Working along the middle line of the next joist, cut out the damaged part of the board with a cross-cut saw.*

3 *Fill a gap with a fillet cut from a spare board and glued in position. Tap it flush with an offcut.*

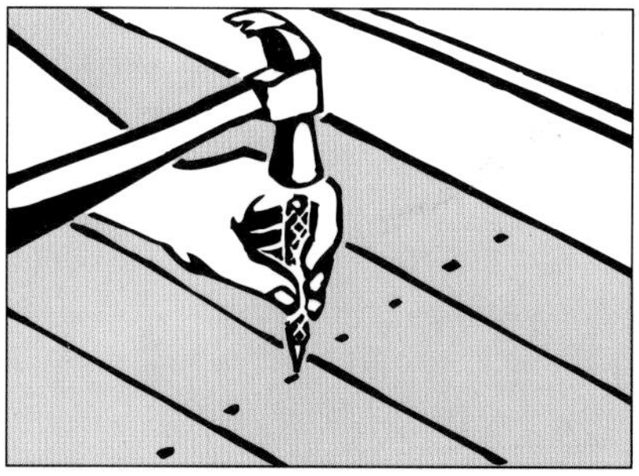

4 *Hammer down all nail heads and tacks that are sticking up from the surface, punching them down if necessary.*

Sanding and cleaning floorboards

▲ *Old pine floorboards here have simply been sanded and sealed. The colour of this type of wood can vary from quite pale to a dark orange: the lighter the shade of the floor, the easier it is to find rugs and other furnishings that work well with the plain unstained wood. The combination here results in an understated and clean look – with a touch of comfort.*

Sanding a floor is usually done using two machines, the larger one to sand the main area of the floor and the smaller one for finishing around the edges. The machines are very noisy and produce a lot of dust, so wear ear defenders and a face mask.

Fix a sheet of coarse paper around the drum of the larger machine; fit it as tightly as possible to reduce the likelihood of it tearing during use. Start the machine with the drum raised above the floor. Begin moving the machine forwards and gently lower the drum so that it comes into contact with the floor before the full weight of the machine is lowered down onto the boards. Raise the drum off the floor gently at the end of a cut. This action will prevent the machine from grinding grooves into the floor. Very uneven or badly cupped boards can be levelled more quickly if sanded diagonally first. Once the boards are level, sand along the boards to remove sanding marks from the diagonal cut; this is a bit like mowing the lawn, just going patiently back and forth. Change the sanding paper from time to time as it will wear and its efficacy will diminish, and empty the dust bag when it is a third full in order to prevent the machine throwing out dust.

When the floor is level fix the same grade of paper onto the edging machine. It is worth noting that this machine tugs away from you, which can be tiring for the back.

Once you have done the edges use the next finest grade of paper on the large machine. It is usually only necessary to make

Using a sanding machine

1 *Tilt the drum off the floor before starting the machine and before each stroke or you will gouge the floorboards.*

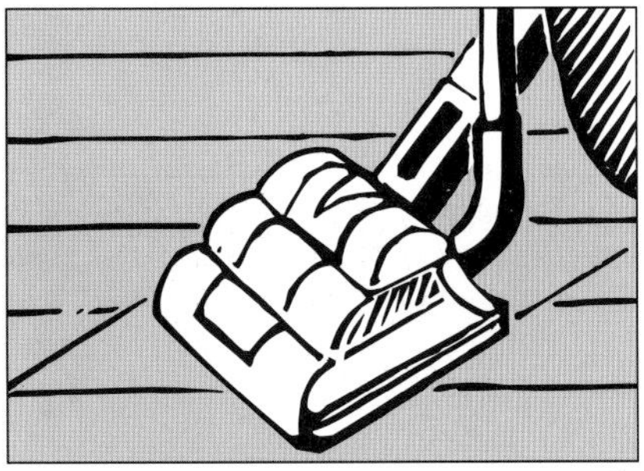

2 *Start by running the machine in diagonal sweeps across the boards with as little overlap as possible.*

3 *Then run the machine along the length of the boards; the process may need to be repeated two or three times.*

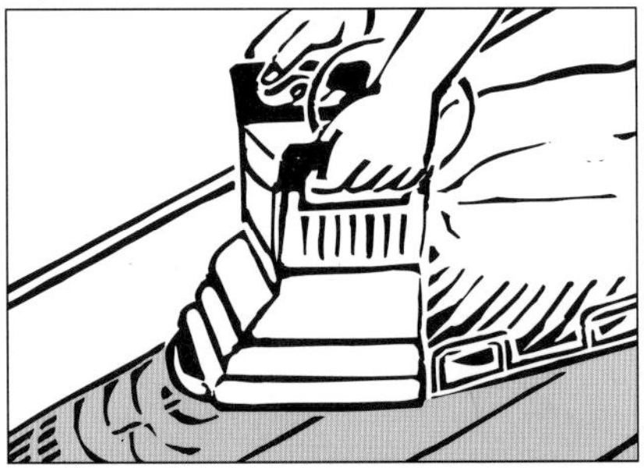

4 *Use an edging sander along the skirting boards, echoing the range of sandpapers used for the main area.*

three or four passes before moving on to the next finest grade. Alternate with the edger using the finer grades of paper in the same way. Finish the corners and other inaccessible areas with an orbital sander or by hand. On previously varnished floors it may be easier to soften the old varnish in the corners with paint stripper before finishing by hand.

Vacuum up the dust and also take some time to suck up dirt from the gaps between the boards, otherwise your paintbrush will pick up the debris during staining, painting or sealing and spoil the finish.

Preparation for painting

Sanding a floor is necessary only for floors in poor condition, or if you intend to use a stain or transparent finish on the wood. For painting, it is possible to scrub the floor clean with water and detergent and lots of elbow grease! The advantage of preparing a floor in this way is that more of the character of the old floor is retained; a few marks, gently bowed boards and uneven grain add charm to the finished look that is more in keeping with older properties.

If a floor has previously been waxed the wax must always be removed, even if the floor is to be sanded, because the machine may melt the wax and force it further into the floor. Using wire wool soaked in white spirit, go over the floor two or three times to make sure no traces of wax remain and finish with a clean rag.

Old paint can be removed chemically or by means of heat. Take care not to scorch the wood if you are using heat to strip off the paint. Sand off any residue by hand.

If the floor is to be finished with opaque colour, you can fill any holes and knocks with a wood filler because this will not show once the floor is painted. Fill the holes and then sand smooth with sandpaper.

▶ *If a pine floor is still too pale after you have sanded it and filled any gaps, it can be stained a warmer, more sympathetic shade, which will make the room less stark. Treating a pine floor in this way can often help to create the naturally darker tone characteristic of oak floorboards.*

Bleaching, liming and staining

Colouring wood grain

Bleaching, liming and staining are decorative treatments that can be applied to wood to alter its colouring without losing the unique quality of the grain. Indeed, on the contrary, bleaching and liming emphasize the wood-grain creating striking effects.

Bleaching

The bleached, greyish floors found in old Scandinavian houses create a subtle, sophisticated background that is perfect for virtually any type of furnishing and colour. Although these floors have been scrubbed over the years to the point where the soft part of the wood is worn away leaving the raised and harder central grain, a similar light and airy feel can be achieved on old boards without quite so much time and effort. It can be done either by bleaching the wood or simply by rubbing white paint into it.

There are a number of chemical wood bleaches available, based on either strong acids or alkalis. Always follow the manufacturer's instructions when using them and ventilate the working environment. Wear protective clothing, rubber gloves and a mask. For further product information request a data sheet from the supplier.

To rub white paint into the wood – be it emulsion or undercoat – is a much simpler operation. Use an old cloth to rub the paint in and wipe off any excess with a clean, dry cloth, finishing in the direction of the grain. Alternatively, you can make up a colourwash with a 1:3 ratio of white emulsion to water. Tint this wash with raw umber and ivory black acrylic colour to make a warm grey, and then add raw sienna to warm the colour further. Test the colour on a board in a discreet corner, allowing it to dry before making any final judgements. If it is too opaque, add more water and adjust the colours to suit.

Both these treatments look best when finished with a matt varnish.

Liming

Limed oak has its origins in the mists of time when oak was a common building material. Coating the oak with lime, a powerful caustic material, prevented attack by wood-boring bugs such as woodworm. It was soon noticed that this treatment created an attractive finish in its own right. Today, benign alternatives to lime are used.

The wood must be sanded back first to its bare state. Then dampen the wood with a cloth and use a fine wire brush to 'rake' out the grain. Do this by moving the brush gently over the surface in the direction of the grain. The idea is to remove the soft porous woody material that naturally fills the grain without scratching the surface of the wood. Clean the debris off with a damp cloth. Then apply a proprietary liming paste, or a runny paste made from titanium dioxide (available from art suppliers) and water, and brush over the whole surface, finishing off by brushing across the grain. Allow the paste to dry. Gently rub off the dried paste using medium-grade wire wool. It should come off the surface but stay in the grain. Gently clean off any powder on the surface with a barely damp sponge. Allow to dry and then varnish.

▲ *Liming a hardwood, such as the ash of this staircase, will transform the natural warm tone of the wood to a cooler, grey colour and will particularly highlight the grain. Thorough preparation of the wood is essential to enable the liming medium to sit in the grain and achieve this distinctive and elegant look.*

Staining

Stains, available in an extensive range of wood shades and brighter colours, effectively alter the colour of wood to tone in with any decorating scheme – without altering its woody appearance. Either use a commercial stain or create your own by adding artist's colour to a varnish that has been diluted by

Liming

1 Having dampened the wood, move a wire brush gently over the surface to 'rake out' the grain.

2 Brush over the whole surface with the liming paste, working with and against the grain, and finally across it.

3 Rub the dried paste gently with wire wool to remove it from the surface, but leaving it in the grain.

4 Take a dampish sponge and clean off any remaining powder from the surface before the varnishing stage.

▲ *Certain woods, such as pine, cannot be limed, because of the characteristics of their grain. Instead, a pine floor such as this can be given the pale quality of limed wood by a process of bleaching. This look particularly suits the airy atmosphere of a room like the one shown here, which is filled with light and furnished in soft tones.*

one third with its appropriate thinner. If you want a very dramatic colour change, though, it is probably easier to use a commercial stain. Colours can be mixed to modify the final shade to suit a particular room. Complex and interesting effects can be created by applying different colours in layers. For example, mahogany stain can sometimes look an artificial purple red but applying a walnut colour over the mahogany will turn it into a rich, warm glow; such a colour could never be achieved by just mixing the two colours together. Try out the colours first on an unwanted scrap piece of wood to ensure that they are right for a particular room; and bear in mind that the same stain can look quite different on different types of wood.

The best way to apply stain is by wiping it on with a rag, working along one board at a time. This will leave a thin colour, so you must build up to the final colour by applying coat after coat until you are happy with the effect. Stains must be protected with varnish, which will bring out the colour of the wood for a deep, glowing effect. If you are using a varnish stain, treat it like varnish and apply it with a brush rather than a rag.

Staining

1 When applying stain to a floor with a rag, work along one board at a time, building up thin layers of colour.

2 Apply varnish stain with a brush, but work back across your floor moving along one board at a time as before.

Painting floors

▶ *This concrete floor has been painted a primrose yellow before being stencilled all over with a geometric repeat pattern. Although the design looks quite complex it is in fact very simple. The advantage of this type of design is that it has no borders to accommodate, making the whole job much easier – from planning to finished floor.*

Painted floors offer the home decorator tremendous scope for choosing colours either to match exactly or to complement other furnishings in the room. The range of commercial colours available is huge and there is an increasing number of so-called historical paint ranges on the market which offer particularly sympathetic and easy-to-live-with hues. In addition, colours can be hand-mixed to offer limitless possibilities. Transparent colours enable you to use quite clear and bright hues that are colourful yet gentle on the eye; a vivid blue that is applied as a diluted wash, for instance, has all the quality of light reflected off water.

Any number of design options provide virtually limitless scope for further improving and manipulating a floor space with paint, allowing for the exercise of personal creative ability. As paint is such a cheap option compared to all the other types of flooring, the only really limiting factor on utilizing the full potential of floors with paint is that of time.

As the choice of designs is so immense, another problem is knowing where to start, what to do. The key to a successful painted floor is to 'keep it simple'. A room with the minimum of plain, simple wooden furniture and neutral fabric colours could have a blaze of deep colour and intricate pattern on the floor as a stunning focal point, but it would be rare. Most rooms have some mixed colours in the form of fabric and furnishings, others are positively cluttered due to small-space city living. For a floor that is to act as a quiet backdrop to the rest of the room, choose neutral tones; introduce one colour, or perhaps at the most two, that match some other colour in the room. Shades of the same colour look very effective together.

A neutral floor can be transformed by the addition of a simple coloured line acting as a border. For example, the floor could be a soft semi-transparent series of cool cream squares divided by mid-oak parquet blocks. The same colours could be used in the border, delineated by two Gustavian green lines; these would 'lift' the whole design and give the border greater definition.

▲ *Instead of using an overall design, you can leave the floor basically plain, and just add a border around the edge. Old boards have been left here in their natural state and a simple border added that picks up on the colour of the doorframe and floorcloth, not only offering decorative interest but also helping to unify several elements in the room.*

Floor areas that have furniture and rugs on them can be broken up by being painted with simple squares, or perhaps be given a *faux*-parquet look for greater visual interest. There are opportunities for simple trompe l'oeil: by setting out painted paving slabs as though they were stepped, for example, thus causing new guests to tread with the same care over the floor as children playing hop-scotch. Furniture that is arranged to form a central focal area can be enlivened by the addition of a design that fits within that area – large stars or circles enclosing a geometric design, say, or an exotic and colourful carpet.

Large and empty hallways offer uncluttered scope for a central design or a more elaborate repeat pattern. Awkward rooms with too many chimney breasts and obtuse corners can be tidied up by running a border in a straight line in front of these obstacles. Borders look better if they are of a generous width, and squares should not be too small and fussy unless you are trying to recreate the look of hand-painted tiles.

Inspiration for designs can be found in books but frequently the room itself provides its own clue: a simple border on a cast-iron fireplace can be adapted; an interesting cornice design can be mirrored in the floor below; or a motif might be taken from a rug. Perhaps a design seen in a musuem or on an expensive item in a shop can be simplified for the floor. Or you could choose a theme such as the seasons as a starting point. Ideas can be related to a particular style: for example, imagery characteristic of Islam would offer considerable scope. Some people have even taken their company logo and used that, or taken ideas related to a particular hobby such as seashell collecting.

If you want to try floor painting, there are many paint techniques from which to choose; those discussed here are a good starting point. Stencilling allows for easily applied repeat patterns or varied arrangements using cut-outs (see pages 22–23). Painting a floor as a chequerboard is dramatic to say the least (see pages 24–25). And creating fake stone and marble effects on floors provides rustic or sophisticated flooring at a fraction of the cost of the real thing (see pages 26–27).

▲ *This floor has been painted to give the impression of a rug that fills the whole floor space; smaller versions that sit in the centre of a room work equally well. Various motifs have been stencilled onto vivid bands of colour, so that the floor becomes an integral part of an exuberant and richly decorated room with highly painted walls and furniture.*

Stencilling

▲ *It is much quicker to execute a complex design with a stencil, and for one like this, it is easier to use a separate stencil for each colour. Aerosol spray paint has been used for this design – quick, but the fumes are unpleasant. Remember, it is not possible to stencil an unbroken line: you will need bridging struts like those at the edge of the central panel here.*

Essentially, a stencil is a template for effectively and quickly transferring a design, even a complex and elaborate one, onto a surface. Each additional colour of the design either requires a separate stencil, or requires one to mask off a different section each time if reusing one stencil for the whole design. Almost any style can be created with stencils.

Borders can vary from delicate natural affairs, with leaves and flowers spilling out onto the main part of the floor, to severely delineated geometric patterns that powerfully define the whole shape of a room.

Stencils are also useful for decorating the main area of a floor. Loose flowing designs can almost blend into each other to provide an overall pattern that is not too overbearing. You can use stencils on top of chequerboard squares. They can even be used to create an intricate chequerboard design or one that incorporates curves and circles. Very small squares or a mosaic type of design can be painted onto a floor in this way with comparative ease.

Specialist shops sell a variety of dedicated stencil paints, but you can easily use your own colours. Acrylic paints are probably the most convenient as they are easy to apply and dry quickly, thereby minimizing the risk of smudging; oil colours, on the other hand, can take days to dry. If the colours are too concentrated, dilute them with the appropriate artist's medium, and remember always to mix sufficient colour at the beginning to complete the job. Standard house decorating paint is too thick and sticky for stencilling.

Stencil designs

There is a comprehensive range of ready-to-use stencil designs on the market – an ever-expanding range – or you can cut your own. Some designs will require little bridging struts to hold the stencil together; you have to paint in the area covered by the struts after the design has been applied. You can mix and match elements from different designs; transfer them into a sketchbook first to see how they will look. It is often useful to do a scale drawing of a design at a more comfortable size before blowing it up on a photocopier to the desired size.

Registration

The purpose of registration is to ensure that the stencil is always placed where it is meant to be and that the second colour is applied in the correct position relative to the first. Draw guidelines in pencil on the floor first. For a border, mark a line the required distance from the skirting board around the room and place the stencil against it as you proceed. An overall pattern will require a grid to keep the stencils correctly spaced.

Registration can be aided by pencilling little marks on the floor corresponding with the exact location of the stencil for each colour; make sure all the stencils are the same size. Ensure that a repeat border has at least one and a half repeats to help with registration, or trace the first design over the second stencil card and match it up at the edges of the painted stencil. Sometimes viewing windows cut in the card are a help.

Cutting the stencil

Stencils need to be waterproof and robust. Oiled card has the advantage of economy and ready availability, but the easiest way of transferring a design onto stencil card is to use transtrace paper. Acetate, a thin clear plastic, is more expensive than card and is not really suitable for intricate designs as it tends to curl up. It is very flexible, though, which means that it bends willingly into awkward corners, unlike card. As acetate is transparent, making sure that the second stencil has been placed exactly over the first part of a design is easy. And transferring the design onto the acetate

Cutting and using a stencil

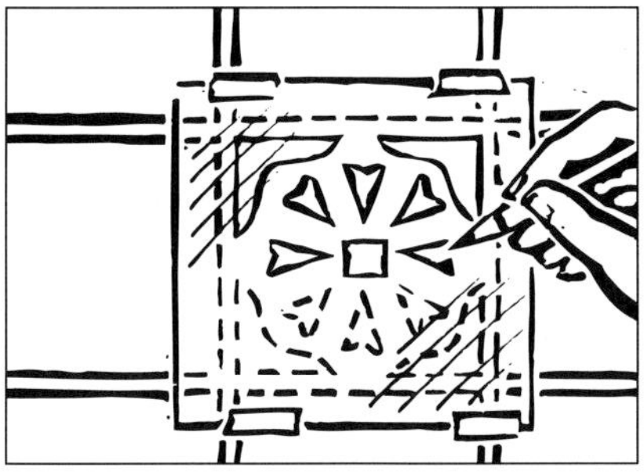

1 Tape your tracing paper in position over the motif you intend to use as a stencil, and carefully copy the outline.

2 Turn the tracing over and tape it in position on a piece of oiled card. Scribble over the outline to transfer it.

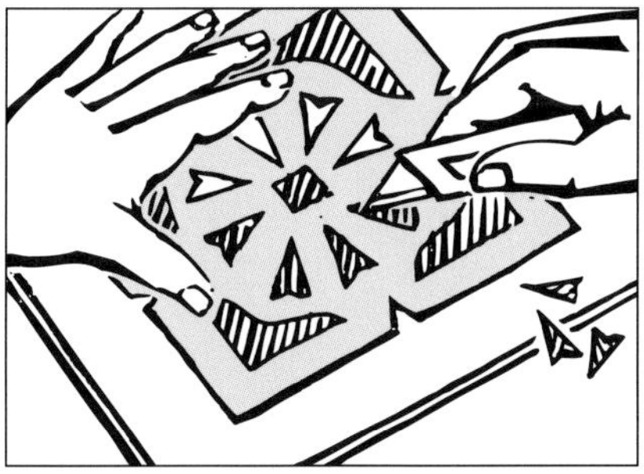

3 With a sharp scalpel, on a board, and remembering to leave bridges,cut out the design and registration marks.

4 Tape the stencil in position, using registration marks; apply the paint slowly, building up the required intensity.

5 When the paint is dry, and checking that the design is complete, carefully peel back and lift off the stencil.

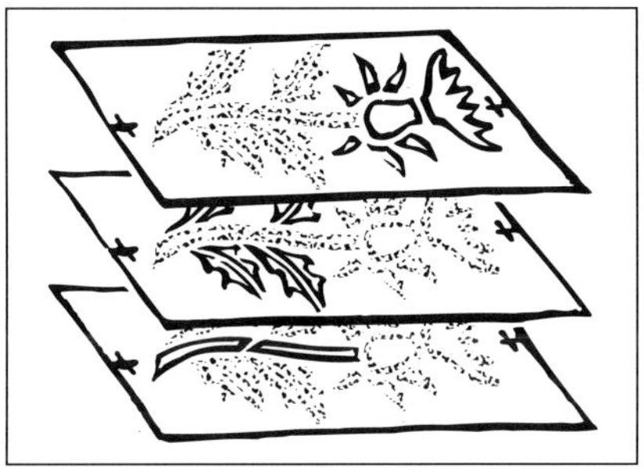

6 For a multi-coloured motif, cut separate stencils for each colour, with dotted guidance lines on each.

7 When re-positioning a border-design stencil, place the stencil in part over the previously painted section.

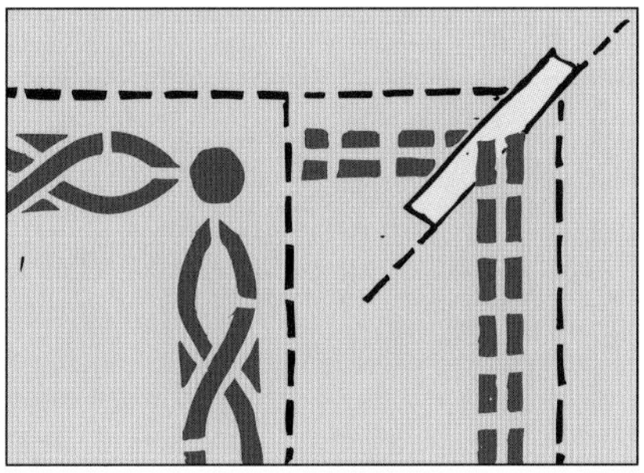

8 At corners, patterns can either be adapted, or mitred – by masking off the approaching patterns at 45 degrees.

is simplicity itself: just tape the acetate to the design and trace the outlines using a fine felt-tipped pen. A thicker, semi-transparent plastic called mylar is now also more widely available: rigid and long-lasting, and facilitating easy registration, this must be an attractive option to consider.

A sharp scalpel is the best tool for cutting out a stencil. Cut it out on either a sheet of glass or a cutting board, taking care not to tear acetate. Card is easier and more satisfying to cut; try to cut it with a bevelled edge towards you. To cut fluently is best, so try to avoid cutting curves in a series of jerks. It is better to stay in a comfortable position and move the stencil as you cut. Cut right into corners, and remember registration marks.

Applying the design

Stick the stencil down with masking tape at the corners so that it cannot move, or spray the back with spray mount which enables the stencil to be peeled up and repositioned several times. Make sure all traces of spray mount are removed from the floor with an appropriate solvent before varnishing.

Use a minimal amount of paint. Dip the tip of the brush into the colour and work it into the brush on some old newspaper or a plate. The brush should appear dry. Stipple the colour over the stencil or brush with a swirling motion so the colour gradually builds up in intensity. Resist the temptation to apply the paint heavily as it invariably seeps under the edge of the stencil. Once the first colour is dry, remove the stencil, then apply a second and further stencils in the same way, using your registration marks as a guide.

Turning corners

Unless they are very linear, border designs do not go around corners so you will need an entirely separate stencil, such as a circle, for the corner. The main pattern finishes just short of the corner and the new stencil is used to fill the space. If the border pattern is to be continuous, lay low-tack masking tape at 45 degrees across the path of the stencil. Work up to and just onto the tape. When it is dry, reposition the tape to the other side of the angle and stencil the other side.

Painting chequerboard squares

Simple squares help break up large spaces and provide the opportunity to introduce two colours to a floor, or two shades of the same colour. And once a simple grid is established the basic alternating squares can be embellished: interspersed stripes could be painted in a variety of arrangements or a stencil design could be added to each square.

With painted squares it is, of course, possible to choose the exact size of the square to suit the scale of the space to be filled. It is easiest to choose a size of square that divides exactly into the floor's area. With a little calculation the squares can be sized to coincide exactly with three walls of any room. In the unlikely event of a perfectly square room, the squares would then fit the fourth wall as well. If you have a number of alcoves, it may be easier – and look better – to paint a central area as a chequerboard and leave a border, in one of the two colours, to stretch to the edges of the room.

Simple squares look more interesting if they are arranged on the diagonal and this is easy to lay out. Begin by setting out the basic grid by following the procedure for setting out tiles (see pages 38–39). Mark out the basic centre point of the floor, adjusting it if necessary, and establish a diagonal line as described. You can work back from this basic central diagonal to mark out the whole room with all the squares on the diagonal. A chalk line is useful for establishing the basic grid but do go over it with pencil as the chalk will rub off as you walk back and forth over the floor. A soft pencil (2B) gives darker, more definite lines that help give the squares sharp edges, useful if your hand tends to wobble as you paint the edges of the squares.

Applying the colour

Painting the squares is simplicity itself. A 2.5cm (1in) brush is the most versatile tool unless the squares are very large, in which case use a 5cm (2in) brush. Thinned transparent – rather than opaque – colour is the easiest to use. Start by the wall furthest from the door and work back towards it, painting every alternate square. Start by outlining your square – some people like to use the brush sideways on to achieve a straight edge. Then

▲ *This hallway has been painted with a simple chequerboard design. The squares have been painted in the same colours as the rest of the woodwork in the room to provide a simple and effective unified scheme, and the skirting board acts as a border for the floor. To reproduce this, paint the whole floor white and then paint the darker colour on as the squares.*

Chequerboard squares

▲ *This kitchen has been painted in the style of classical tiling. The alternating squares are painted in a slightly darker shade to differentiate between them (in the absence of grout). The border has been painted in a bold green, along with most of the key squares – though the odd one or two are red, for fun and additional interest.*

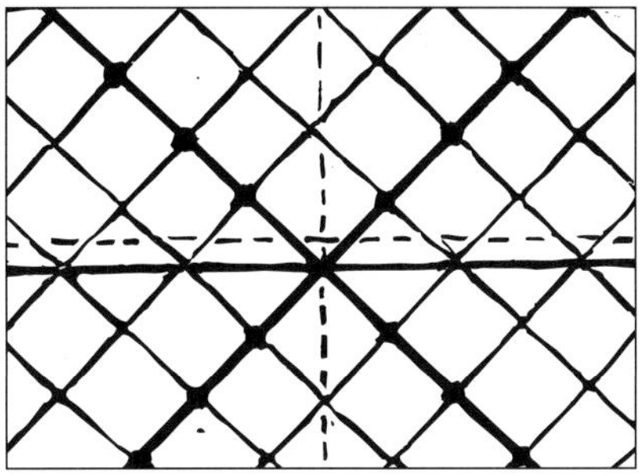

***1** Find and adjust the centre point of your floor as necessary and mark out all the squares on the diagonal.*

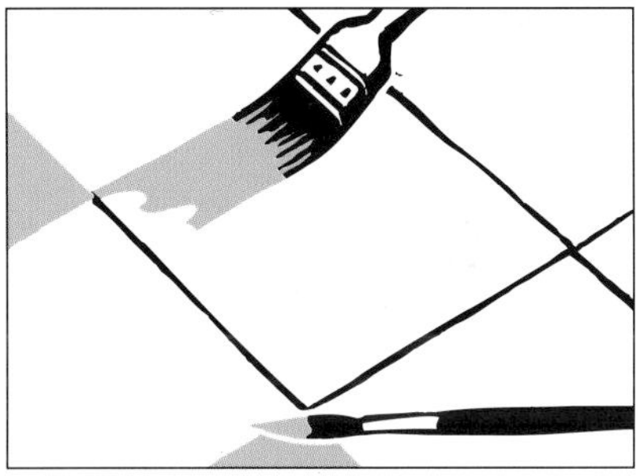

***2** Paint the whole floor in one colour, then the second colour in alternate squares. Begin by outlining your square.*

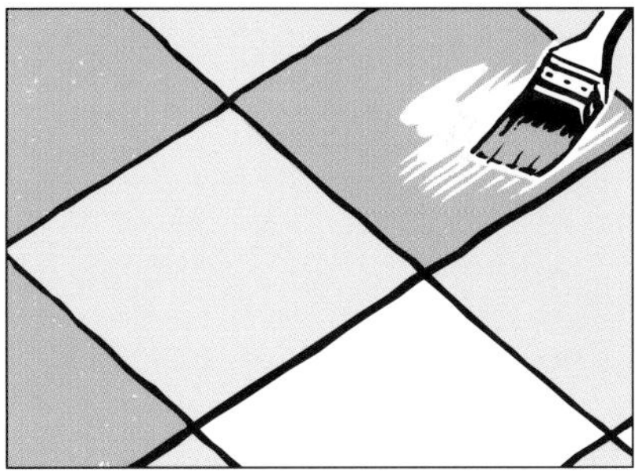

***3** Having created sharp corners with a fine artist's brush, block in the centre of the outlined square.*

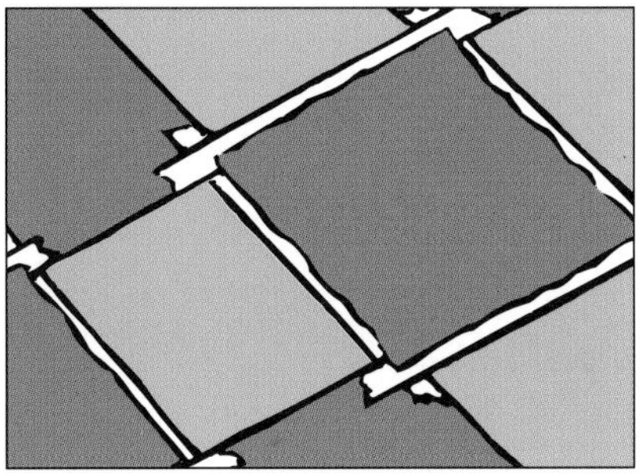

***4** Masking tape makes sharp edges easier; but it can be confusing, so be sure to paint only alternate squares.*

use an artist's brush to colour in the apex of each corner. Finish by blocking in the centre of each square. When all the first colour is finished and dry, repeat the process for the alternating squares in the second colour. If you are using opaque colour it will be necessary to prime and undercoat the floor first, then to paint the whole floor with the lighter of the two chequerboard colours and finally to paint on the darker colour as alternating squares. If the first coat of the second colour does not cover satisfactorily in one coat you will have to go over the paint again when it has dried. For sharper edges (or if your hand is very unsteady), mask out the outline of every alternate square with low-tack masking tape, and brush colour over the edges.

Wood stain colours can be used on bare wood for a quick effect. Score along the pencil lines with a sharp scalpel. Paint wood stain as close to the line as you can. The stain will bleed into the wood, rather like ink spilt onto blotting paper, but will stop neatly on the scored line preventing further colour spread. When the colour is fully dry, protect the floor with varnish or lacquer.

Painting *faux*-stone effects

Real marble and stone floors are beyond the means of most people but can be imitated easily and cheaply using paint. Stone-effect techniques look very convincing as they are rarely examined close to; being on such a large scale, the eye takes in an impression rather than focusing on detail. Use painted stone effects where the genuine material would be used. For example, a hallway can be given a palatial air by painting alternating black-and-white *faux*-marble squares or coloured-marble panels over the whole floor. For floors in poor condition, or if you find the texture of cement or chipboard unforgiving, a covering layer of plywood will provide a more sympathetic surface.

The paint techniques used here rely on scumble glaze, a transparent medium that is designed to have colour added to it to create texture for decorative effects such as rag

▲ *Real stone flagstones and plywood squares painted to resemble stone are effectively juxtaposed in this hallway. The floorboards originally beyond the stone were in poor condition; now the gaps between the 'stones' have been grouted for maximum effect and the whole scheme pulls together very happily – with no ugly junctions.*

Creating a *faux*-marble effect

1 *Lay plywood squares as flagstones. Leave gaps for grout between the squares to strengthen the illusion.*

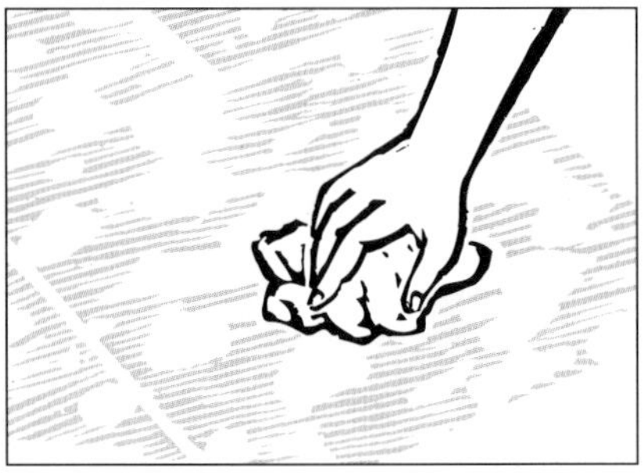

2 *Apply the base coat and leave it to dry. Paint on the glaze and use a rag to break up and mottle the surface.*

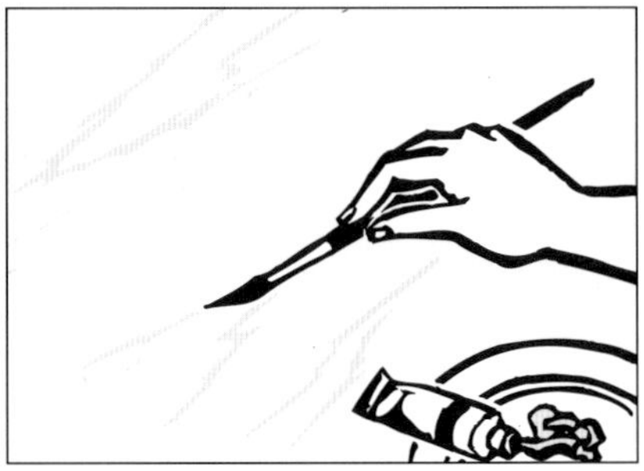

3 *With a fine artist's brush, fidget the veins onto the wet glaze, keeping the movement in one overall direction.*

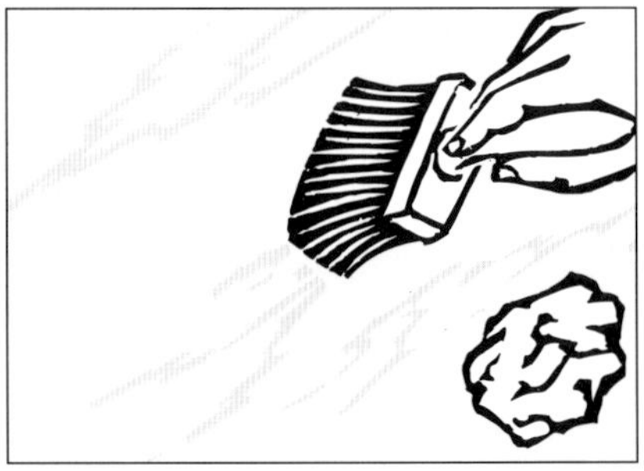

4 *Soften the veins with a soft brush in the direction of the veins, then backwards and then with the grain again.*

rolling and stippling. Slow-drying, and normally diluted with white spirit before use, it is applied over an eggshell base paint. As it has a marked tendency to yellow, take care when using it for pale colours. The addition of a little white undercoat helps to minimize the yellowing. Scumble glaze has to be given a coat of varnish for protection.

Installing plywood 'stones'

Plywood is generally sold as 2.44 x 1.22m (8 x 4ft) sheets, but you can ask your timber merchant to saw these up for you into smaller, more appropriately sized squares – say, 60 x 60cm (2 x 2ft) – to create a chequerboard or flagstone effect. Provided the floor is reasonably level, plywood 6mm (¼in) thick is sufficient.

Allow the boards to acclimatize for 48 hours in the room before laying them, and then lay the plywood following the guidelines for laying tiles (see pages 56–57). If you leave a gap between the squares, you can fill it with a flexible grout or coloured filler reinforced with PVA adhesive to carry further the illusion of a stone floor. Fix the plywood onto concrete using panel adhesive or onto wood surfaces using small panel pins. Prime and paint the plywood and finish with two coats of white eggshell, an ideal base for subsequent paint finishes.

Faux marble

For a simple and discreet finish, marble the floor using one base colour, perhaps with a darker shade for veining. For a darker and more dramatic looking marble, use a dark base colour and light veining. For alternating chequerboard squares or inlaid panels choose two contrasting base colours, either very dark and light squares or a neutral background colour combined with a brighter, more vivid hue.

Find some examples of real marble and copy the colours and the style. Due to the large areas involved, marbling on floors is best kept simple; you are trying to create an impression of the real material rather than a slavish copy. The secret is to get the veining right; once you develop the feel for veining you are almost there.

Oil-based paints make marbling easier. Start by mixing up the base coat as a glaze with 50 per cent scumble glaze and 50 per cent white spirit to the consistency of single cream. For pale grey marble add some white artist's oil colour or undercoat and mix in thoroughly. Mix in a little ivory black; this is a very powerful colour so add only a little at a time. If the colour seems like a thin black rather than a creamy grey add more white until the balance is right. Check the colour on the floor; samples can easily be cleaned off with a little white spirit.

Paint the base colour over an area about 60cm (2ft) square or, ideally, a whole 'paving stone' at a time. Break up the glazed surface with a rag so it becomes mottled. Use artist's oil paints as veining colour, squeezed onto a plate and diluted with a little white spirit to provide a more workable consistency. A very fine artist's brush is ideal for veining. Fidget the veins onto the wet glaze; marble has an overall direction and the veins are angular rather than rounded. Veins never stop abruptly, they either gradually fade into the rock or join other veins. Do not overdo the veining. The last thing you want is something that looks like a road map. Dab off any excess paint from the veins with a rag. So that they become blurry at the edges, soften and blend the veins using a hogs'-hair softener, a very fine-bristled brush available from decorating shops, or, if you are on a tight budget, a decorator's dusting brush. Soften in the direction of the veins first, then lightly against the veins to spread them a little. Finish off by softening with the veins. Allow the paint to dry thoroughly before applying varnish.

Faux limestone

A warm, creamy limestone is the essence of restrained good taste yet can be imitated with paint for a fraction of the cost of the real thing. A floor painted as stone is an imposing yet quiet backdrop that harmonizes well with almost any decorating scheme.

Mix up the base coat as a glaze with 50 per cent scumble glaze and 50 per cent white spirit to the consistency of single cream, using raw sienna and plenty of white undercoat as the colouring, and then add a little raw umber to 'dirty' the colour. The objective is to mix a pale yet warm cream. Paint the base colour over an area about 60cm (2ft) square or, ideally, a whole 'paving stone' at a time. Stipple the surface to break the colour up into millions of tiny flecks. Use a stippling brush or improvise with a 5cm (2in) brush. Allow the paint to dry.

The second application consists of a light and a dark version of the same colour, to give the 'stone' the appearance of age and wear. Use a well-thinned scumble glaze or a diluted oil-based varnish. Mix some raw umber and a little black to create a dirty colour that takes the edge off the cream. Make up two shades of the same colour, one dark and one pale, for a variable effect. Paint random patches of the two colours together and stipple as you did for the first colour. Use a greater proportion of the darker colour where the floor is subjected to greater wear, near a door, for example, for authenticity.

Creating a *faux*-stone effect

1 Paint on the glaze and then stipple the surface to break up the colour into flecks. Leave this coat to dry.

2 Brush on lighter and darker versions of the same colour in random patches, and then stipple them as before .

Varnishing, lacquering and waxing

▲ *This floor has been finished with a satin varnish, which often looks more flattering than its more familiar high-gloss equivalents. Satin varnish also has the advantage of creating a less slippery surface than gloss; this can be important in a room such as this, where a large floor area is exposed, and especially in a house where there are young children.*

Varnishing

1 Apply the varnish generously with a brush, working along the length of a couple of boards at a time.

2 When re-varnishing a floor, you must first clean the surface: use wire wool, water and a sugar soap solution.

Most decorative floor treatments need additional protection against the battering of countless feet and becoming faded and grey. Sealing the floor with a clear varnish or lacquer will ensure that the floor will continue to look good, last, and remain easy to clean for many years.

Wax, the time-honoured way of protecting floors, builds up an organic layer which protects the floor, smells pleasant and has a rich, deep shine that is renewed every time the floor is re-waxed, providing protection indefinitely. Plain wood floors look particularly good when waxed, because the wax provides a warm mellow colour that appears entirely natural – unlike the more plastic quality of modern lacquers.

Varnishing

Oil- and water-based varnishes can be used straight out of the container but must be stirred thoroughly before use. Oil-based varnish dries slowly, so sealing a floor will take days rather than hours. Acrylic varnish is recoatable after 2 hours, which speeds things up considerably.

If you do use an acrylic varnish, ensure that you use one specifically formulated for floors because the ordinary varnishes are not as hard-wearing as some of the solvent-based products. It is worth checking too that it will not react with any existing floor coatings. Oil paints can take days – if not weeks – to cure properly, and uncured oil paint can cause acrylic varnish to craze.

Start in the corner furthest from the door and brush the varnish on fairly generously, but working along only a couple of boards at a time. When the first coat has dried, apply the second coat in the same way. You should continue to apply varnish until you have a minimum of three coats in low-traffic areas and as many as five coats in rooms that will receive major wear and tear.

Revarnishing

If you are re-finishing a previously varnished floor, you will first have to roughen the surface and dislodge deeply ingrained dirt using medium-grade wire wool and water. Then, using a sugar-soap solution, clean the surface again to remove any remaining grease and wipe clean with a damp cloth. If you are working with newly painted or stained floors, you will only need to vacuum to remove the dust from the floor. If the room has been sanded, ensure that all the walls and any other surfaces are dust-free before varnishing. Open all the windows, as solvent-based products give off strong fumes which can be harmful.

Unless it is very cold outside, a draught will help the sealer to dry more quickly. For a super-smooth finish, sand the sealer with a fine-grade silicon carbide paper before applying the final coat.

▲ *Floors in bathrooms should be sealed with particular care in order to prevent the wood becoming waterlogged. This floor is finished with a matt varnish, the most discreet of floor finishes. Although matt finishes should be avoided in areas of heavy wear, the effect here is subtle and elegant, and, given the appropriate care, the varnish will survive many years.*

Lacquering

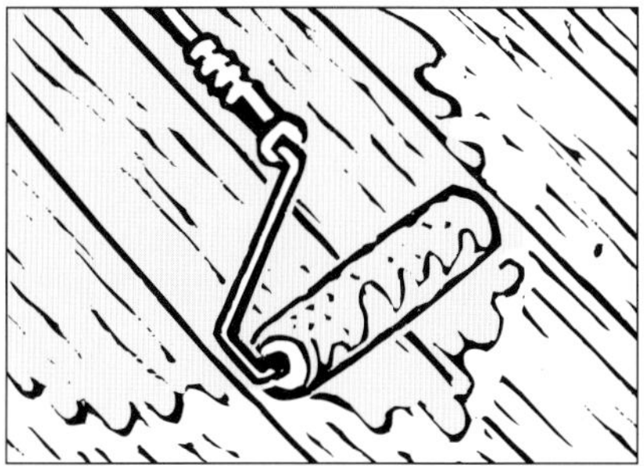

1 Work with enough 'mixed' lacquer to cover a quarter of the floor; spread it on quickly , and as thickly as possible.

Waxing

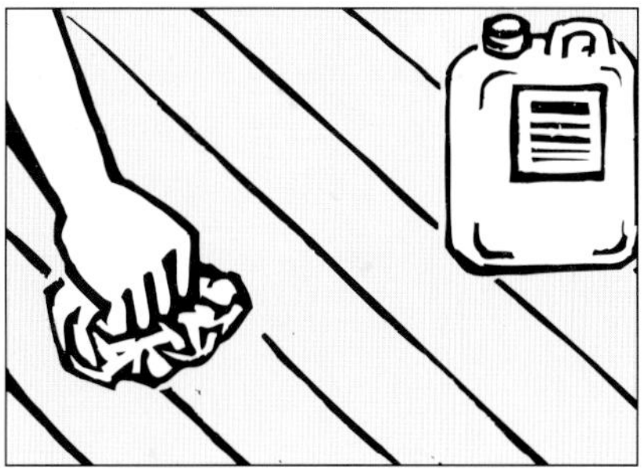

1 Apply floor wax with a dry cloth. When it is dry, and regularly thereafter, buff it up with a cloth.

Lacquering

Floor lacquers usually consist of two components: the bulk of the product, often sold in 5 litre (1 gallon) containers, and a special hardener or crosslinker that must be mixed with the lacquer before use. Always follow the manufacturer's instructions. And because, once mixed, it must be used within a limited time, calculate how much lacquer will be needed before you mix it (see pages 14–15).

Shake the main component thoroughly in its container and, working to the nearest litre (⅕ gallon), pour enough for the job into a paint kettle. Pour in the appropriate amount of hardener and stir with a small brush. Wait for 5 minutes before using it.

The lacquer can be brushed on in the same way as varnish except that it should be laid on as thickly as possible. Ideally you should use a special lambswool mop, though a roller fitted with an extension handle may be more effective for large areas. Simply pour enough lacquer from the container directly onto the floor and use the roller to distribute it evenly. Several square metres (yards) can be covered at a time. If there are gaps in the floorboards, load the roller from a tray to prevent losing too much lacquer through the gaps. Depending on conditions, floor lacquer can be recoated after 1–2 hours. Three coats are sufficient for most domestic situations.

Waxing

Sanded floors that are to be waxed should be sealed first with a coat of polyurethane varnish, or a sand-and-seal shellac, to prevent the wax from sinking into the wood. Use a wax specially formulated for floors.

Apply the wax with a cloth, then leave it for 1 hour before polishing it off with a clean dry cloth. Finish by buffing up the wax to a shine with a soft cloth. Re-apply wax as frequently as once a week for high-wear areas such as kitchens; most rooms, though, only need waxing once every few months.

Manufacturers of wood-strip flooring also supply special water-based waxes that can be used to provide additional protection for lacquered floors. These can be brushed or sprayed on and either buffed up when dry or simply left as they are.

Laying new flooring

Because flooring materials are so varied, laying a new floor may involve anything from a few hours of easy work – involving a few basic tools and common sense – to a major upheaval requiring specialized knowledge and equipment, and a serious commitment in terms of time and energy. Before embarking on a project yourself, take time to examine what is really the appropriate solution, and ponder the practical and aesthetic ramifications of your choice before making a final decision.

The first step is to establish what the existing floor is constructed of. Peel back coverings such as carpet or vinyl to see what is underneath. It is worth checking in more than one place, as it is not unusual to have a cement floor and a suspended timber floor in the same room. Look carefully, because things are not always as they seem. Plain floorboards, for instance, although usually indicative of a suspended wood floor, could also be wood-strip flooring laid over concrete or chipboard.

Next, you have to establish what type of flooring can be laid over the existing floor. Most materials can be laid over all types of floor but in some cases adequately preparing the subfloor can involve additional costs. Most types of flooring can be laid quickly and easily, although some jobs are more complicated than others. It is generally more disruptive, for instance, to lay hard floors (see pages 40–47), than flexible (see pages 48– 57) or wood (see pages 58–63) floors. Be prepared for some mess and inconvenience.

Once you know what sort of flooring you are dealing with, you can then decide on what type of floor-covering you prefer and whether it is going to be practical for the situation. Jute flooring looks sophisticated in the right setting, for instance, but is not suitable for a bathroom where water is splashed around. Disappointment will set in quickly when the jute starts to turn black and rot, and deep frustration will soon follow when it is discovered that there is no satisfactory way of cleaning it.

The next stage is to assess the affordability of your preferred material. Measure the room and estimate how much is needed of the product in question (see pages 36–37).

◀ *Laying wood-strip flooring is one of the easiest DIY flooring tasks. Wood floors are also extremely versatile, as they can be laid over most types of subfloor. Wood provides a very practical and easy-to-clean surface, which is particularly important in a dining room like this, where it is likely that food and wine will be spilled.*

▲ *Laying flagstones is the most difficult and disruptive flooring project it is possible to undertake, but the floor will last for ever once it is finished. These polished limestone flags might seem like an unusual choice for a bedroom but in fact work well with the clean lines and warm tones of the fitted furniture.*

Shop around to find out all the costs involved. Some materials span a wide price band. For example, carpet can be one of the cheapest or one of the most expensive floor-coverings – depending upon quality and type. Some flooring materials are so expensive that it may be worth paying a professional that little bit extra to ensure that the end result justifies the overall cost. Other materials are cheap to buy but expensive to have laid, and, provided you feel sufficiently confident and have the spare time, these are well worth laying yourself. There is also the satisfaction to be derived from working through for oneself from the first glimmer of an idea to the actual creation of the finished scheme.

Fitting might be included in the price, although 'free fitting' is rarely what it claims to be. See what the ancillary costs are, such as underlay and gripper strips or special tile adhesive needed for a problem floor. The savings made by installing the floor yourself may enable you to buy a more expensive material. Check also to see if costly tools are needed to do the job and whether these can be hired (see pages 36–37). Read the relevant sections in this chapter to decide whether you feel sufficiently confident to install the flooring yourself.

Having established which is the most suitable floor-covering, check on availability and delivery times. Most products can be delivered in a week but sometimes a special order is required and delivery can take something like six weeks. Now is the time to obtain the fixing materials and any special tools needed for the job. Either buy them or book the hire of an expensive tool.

A few days before the due delivery date remove the old floor-covering and repair or prepare the existing subfloor. Concrete, chipboard or floorboards may need some attention, dips and bumps to be levelled or cracks to be filled, before new flooring can safely be laid on them (see pages 34–35).

It may be necessary to acclimatize the new material to its new environment for a day or two before laying it in order to ensure a successful job (see pages 26–27, 34–35). Before tiling a floor you will need to mark out guidelines against ▷

which to work. Although the principles are the same for any type of tile, the starting points are adjusted according to whether the room is square, rectangular or irregular (see pages 38–39).

Concrete floors

Concrete might seem an ugly and unforgiving material but, in fact, it provides a perfect base for all types of floor-covering, as long as it is smooth and level. Carpets (see pages 68–69) and wood flooring (see pages 62– 63) are easily laid over concrete. It is also an ideal base for tiles (see pages 44–47) and is really the only material with the structural integrity required for laying very heavy materials such as flagstones and brick (see pages 42–43), making it almost invaluable.

Chipboard and plywood floors

These floors are constructed in the same way as traditional suspended timber floors except that boards of chipboard or plywood are used to cover the joists instead of floorboards. They have been commonly installed in housing since the 1960s because of the increasing cost of traditional materials and because man-made boards are easy to lay and very stable. They are also found in older properties where rotten boards have been replaced. Both chipboard and plywood are perfect as subfloor surfaces for most types of floor-covering because they are very smooth and level. Take care when laying very heavy materials over any type of suspended wood floor, however, as the joists might need to be reinforced to take the extra weight.

▲ Concrete floors are commonly found in newer houses and blocks of flats and can be covered with most flooring materials. Floors as smooth and level as that illustrated here can be easily painted, providing a stylish and economical finish for what is often considered an ugly and difficult raw material.

▶ Newer and renovated properties often have chipboard and plywood laid over joists, and this can either make a good base for other materials or be painted easily. At the bottom of the stairs here plywood has been laid as large squares and painted black, so that its appearance is almost indistinguishable from polished slate.

▲ *Provided that the boards are waterproofed first, wooden decking can be used to define the space occupied by a freestanding bath in a bathroom, and is both a practical and smart design solution. Thin tiles have been carefully laid over well-prepared old floorboards on the rest of the floor, creating an interesting variety of texture in a monochrome room.*

Suspended timber floors

Although pine floorboards are one of the most attractive types of flooring in their own right, they need greater preparation than some other materials before certain types of floor-covering can be laid over them. Wood-strip flooring (see pages 62–63) can be laid directly over floorboards if they are reasonably level. Before laying carpet (see pages 68–69) or flexible floor-coverings (see pages 48–51), however, a hardboard base needs to be installed (see pages 34–35). Tiles can be laid directly onto boards as long as they are level and reasonably rigid and you use a flexible adhesive; otherwise you can lay 12mm (½in) plywood sheets over the floorboards to provide the necessary rigidity. Special underlays and flexible tile adhesives that eliminate the need for laying plywood are now available; consult your tile supplier. Many stones and slates are available in a thinner tile format which can be laid over timber floors, but thick traditional flagstones should always be laid on a solid base.

Preparing surfaces

Before you lay any new floor-covering, you will need to check that the floor is in good enough condition to receive it. Generally, most flooring requires a smooth, even surface that is free from cracks, dips and bumps. Some may require a new intermediate surface to be installed over the existing sub-floor; it is worth estimating for this before you start, as not only could this hidden cost be a nasty shock if revealed as a necessity halfway through the job, it could actually have an effect on the type of floor-covering you can afford to choose.

Concrete floors

Laying any type of flooring on concrete requires a smooth and level surface – with the possible exception of materials that are bedded on mortar or thick-bed adhesives. Concrete floors are normally finished with a sand-and-cement screed laid over the coarse cement base, and they should incorporate a damp-proof membrane.

Check the level of any dampness present using a moisture meter. If the levels are higher than those specified by the manufacturer for the type of floor-covering to be laid, a damp-proof layer must be added before you begin work. This membrane can either take the form of a polythene sheet or a bitumen waterproofer which would be brushed onto the concrete base.

Special precautions may have to be taken if the floor incorporates underfloor central heating. Tile adhesives may require the use of special additives, and with wood floors allow plenty of room for expansion.

Filling cracks

Cracks in concrete floors are a common problem and are easily repaired with mortar. First rake out and widen the cracks with a bolster chisel and hammer, then dampen the area to be repaired with water.

Mix sand and cement in a 3:1 ratio with water to form a workable mixture and press the mortar into the cracks using a trowel. Smooth the surface level, and allow the repair a few days to dry before you start to lay the new floor-covering.

▲ *This concrete floor has been sanded and polished to provide a tough and practical surface that seems more than appropriate in this modern interior. Obviously, a floor in as good a condition as this would need no further preparation were it to be hidden under some sort of covering – whether for practical or aesthetic reasons.*

Preparing concrete floors

1 *Using a trowel, fill the dampened crack with mortar. Smooth level and leave for a few days to dry thoroughly.*

2 *Self-levelling compound is applied as a runny paste to a dampened floor. Leave it to find its own level and dry.*

Sealing the surface

Concrete floors that are very dusty with the top layer flaking off as a powder should be treated with a concrete sealer or with a PVA general-purpose builder's sealer, diluted with water according to the manufacturer's instructions.

Levelling with compound

Unevenness in concrete floors caused by lots of cracks and shallow depressions less than 3mm (⅛in) deep can be rectified with a self-levelling compound obtainable from builders' merchants. Dampen the floor with water before starting work. Mix the compound with water to form a runny paste. Starting at the corner furthest from the door, trowel the mixture onto the floor to a depth of 3mm (⅛in) using a float. Leave the compound to find its own level and harden off; the floor-covering can be laid the following day.

Wood floors

Replacing chipboard and plywood boards

There is very little that can go wrong with chipboard and plywood floors: damp or leaks, however, can cause chipboard to disintegrate and plywood to swell. If you find that damage has ocurred, simply lever up the damaged board and replace it with a new piece cut to the same size as the original.

If you are aware that noise is likely to be a problem in the room below you, lay a sound-deadening material between the existing surface and the new one when you are laying wood-strip or flexible flooring.

Pine floorboards

Boards that have become very cupped with age or that have large gaps between them will ruin virtually all types of new floor covering. Carpets and vinyl will wear on the ridges, ceramic tiles will crack and wood-strip floors will creak and lurch continually unless action is taken. Individual damaged boards can be replaced (see pages 14–15) but an uneven floor should be entirely covered with a layer of hardboard or, if it is in really poor condition, thin plywood, which is more rigid.

Laying hardboard and plywood boards

The same technique can be employed for both hardboard and plywood although there are slight differences in the way they are fixed. Both types of board are normally sold as 2.44 x 1.22m (8 x 4ft) sheets but are easier to handle and to lay if they are cut smaller. Ask your supplier to cut them in half so that you end up with squares with sides of 1.22m (4ft). Allow the boards to acclimatize for 48 hours in the relevant room before laying them. Hardboard can even be dampened with water to allow it to settle more evenly.

In a regularly shaped room, start laying the sheets against the longest, straightest wall and work towards the opposite wall. In an irregularly shaped room, begin in the centre and work outwards; find the centre as you would before tiling a floor (see pages 38–39).

Lay the boards so that the middle of each new sheet adjoins the bottom of the join between the two previously laid sheets, rather like a brick wall. Use small nails, no longer than 18mm (¾in) long, at 15cm (6in) intervals, to fix plywood boards. If laying 12mm (½in) plywood for hard tiles, screw the boards down at 30cm (12in) intervals.

Hardboard should be laid with the rough side facing upwards. Nail it to the floorboards from the centre outwards in a radial pattern so it does not buckle. Space the nails at 15cm (6in) intervals but 10cm (4in) apart at the edges of the sheets. This is less critical for plywood, which is much more rigid.

Determine where to cut the edging boards by placing them (upside-down and with one edge against the skirting board) over the last of the laid boards. Using a pencil, mark where the edges of the bottom boards touch the top ones. Cut the boards at these points using a saw and fix them into position the right way up. This technique only works if the edge of the board against the skirting is cut square. If you are using an offcut as an edging piece, ensure that the uncut, square end of the offcut is against the skirting board. Use a profile gauge (see pages 36–37) to transfer the profile of architraves onto the board so that it can be cut to fit, and stop the boards against the doorstop.

Laying hardboard

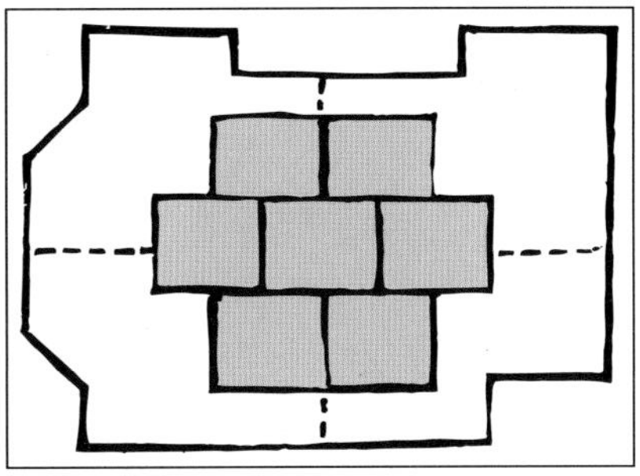

1 In an irregularly shaped room, establish your centre point and work outwards, laying the boards like bricks.

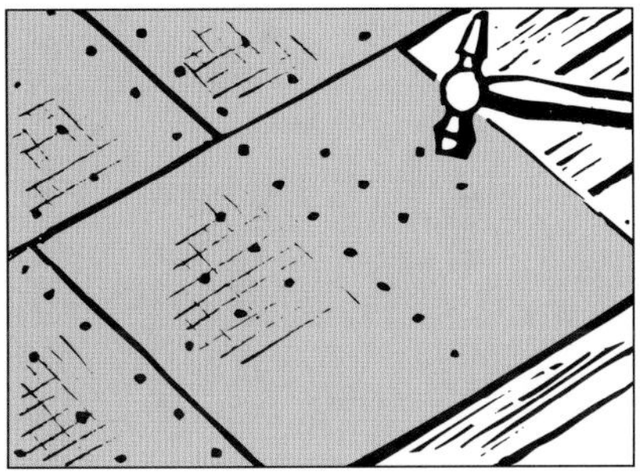

2 Secure the boards with short nails, working in a radial pattern, and with more nails going in at the edges.

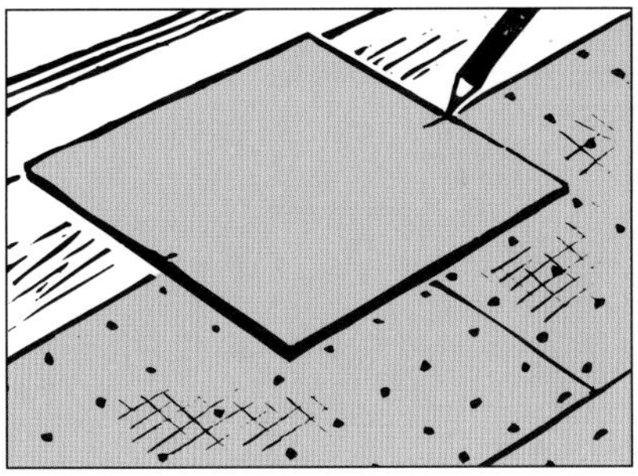

3 Simply turn a board upside-down and mark an overlap in order to cut board to fit exactly at the room's edge.

4 Use a profile gauge to produce an accurate pattern to cut when it comes to door frames and the like.

Estimating and equipment

▲ *It is wise not to over-order expensive materials lilke the ash flooring here, so draw a scale plan of the room, taking particular care to be accurate if, as in this case, the room is an irregular shape with obstructions such as curved-edge stairs to work into the calculation. Underestimating is equally frustrating, and can lead to poor colour matches.*

Ordering the right amount of material is vital to ensure that there is sufficient to finish the job neatly. This is particularly important with flexible sheet materials in order to avoid having to make unnecessary ugly seams and because of the risk of colour variations between different batches of material. Whilst over-ordering is simply a waste of money, it is nonetheless essential to order slightly more than you calculate you will need to compensate for the inevitable wastage that arises when you are working around obstacles, and from mistakes and breakages. It is unlikely, for example, that you will be able to find a place for all the half-tiles left as offcuts when you tile the border of a room. Obviously, it is crucial to estimate as accurately as possible to minimize wastage, and to estimate accurately you must measure accurately. Take your time; double-check measurements and sums; and you will probably save both time and money.

Measuring up

It is always worth taking an accurate plan of your room to your supplier, who will know the best way to save material – particularly in awkwardly shaped rooms. However, rooms with square or rectangular walls without any interruptions along them are easy to measure. And to calculate the area, simply establish the width and depth of the room and multiply one figure by the other; this is the number of square metres (yards) to be covered. Most rooms have various obstacles, however: built-in cupboards, chimney breasts and alcoves. In order to include these in your estimate, first measure the width and depth of the unobstructed rectangle forming the room's central part, and calculate that area. Then measure the width and depth of every recess and add these together to calculate the total area occupied by these recesses. Finally add this figure to the first figure to calculate the

Tools and equipment

General tools

In addition to everyday tools, some more specialized implements will be required for preparing surfaces and laying floor-coverings. The more general of these are described below, but task-specific tools will be explained in the relevant sections of this chapter.

- **Straight edge:** length of metal used to ensure edges or lines are straight. Also useful for checking tiles are laid level, and joining up points with a straight line.
- **Chalk line:** length of string that pulls out from a unit rather like a tape measure except that it coats the line with a coloured chalk. Used for marking out straight lines on a large scale. The string is stretched taut between two points and plucked against the surface leaving a line of chalk.
- **Club hammer:** heavy hammer used when brute force is needed. An ideal partner for the bolster chisel.
- **Bolster chisel:** large, blunt, flat-bladed metal chisel useful for tasks as diverse as levering up floorboards, breaking heavy tiles and stone in two and laying carpet.
- **Try square:** used to mark a line at 90 degrees to an edge and for marking the line of a right-angled corner.
- **Trimming knife:** bulky handle holding sharp blade that can be changed when it becomes blunt. Used for cutting flexible materials, such as cork or vinyl, and carpet.
- **Craft knife:** smaller and sharper than a trimming knife. Particularly useful for cutting stencils from oiled card.
- **Trowel:** used for repairs to concrete floors: for mixing small quantities of cement, filling cracks and final smoothing of the repair.
- **Float:** smoothing tool used for screeding. Use a metal plasterer's float for spreading self-levelling compound.
- **Profile gauge:** a series of metal pins that pass through a holder. The gauge is pressed against any intricate areas and the pins are displaced in the shape of the profile. Useful for measuring the profile of architraves when cutting flexible flooring materials.

actual area of floor space to be covered – in square metres (yards). In a trapezoid room, there is really no alternative but to draw a plan to scale on graph paper.

Flexible flooring

For flexible sheet materials you need to order enough material to fit between the two widest dimensions of the room, as the excess is simply trimmed away from any obstructions to avoid making unnecessary seams. Large areas of trimmed material can often be used elsewhere but try to tuck seams away in an unobtrusive corner. Seams should run at 90 degrees to a window as they are less visible in that position. Sheet materials are available in various widths so ensure that the sum of the widths is the same as or greater than the width of the room. The total length of material required is the number of widths required, allowing for pattern-matching and wastage, multiplied by the length of the room.

Tiles

Calculate how many of your tiles are required per square metre and multiply that number by the number of square metres in the room. Remember that you will have to cut tiles to fit at the edges. Estimate the number of extra tiles you will need by allowing enough to tile one additional strip along half the walls and then add a few more in case of breakages. With larger, more expensive tiles it may be worth calculating if offcuts can be used to prevent waste. Your final figure will have to be rounded up – tiles are supplied in boxes – so you will probably have tiles left over.

Wood-strip flooring

Calculate how many strips of the desired planking are needed to fit the width of the room. Multiply the number of strips by the length of the room to calculate the total length required. Allow a little extra for cutting as there are bound to be a few short lengths that will be unusable. Pre-finished flooring is sold by the box so your final figure will have to be rounded up to the nearest number of complete boxes.

Tools and equipment

For wood floors

- **Cross-cut saw:** long saw for general-purpose wood-cutting across the grain, normally used for cutting floorboards to length.
- **Ripsaw:** long saw with large, widely spaced teeth for cutting wood along the grain, most often necessary when the last board in a floor is too wide.
- **Tenon saw:** small handsaw with a reinforced back to prevent the blade from flexing and very fine teeth for intricate work.
- **Floor saw:** saw with a curved cutting edge to enable a floorboard to be cut without damaging the boards on either side.
- **Coping saw:** thin blade supported by large metal frame for cutting curves in wood, normally used if a floorboard needs shaping to fit around an obstacle.
- **Chisel:** tool with a very sharp blade, available in various widths. Useful for cutting where a saw cannot be used. Used in conjunction with a wooden mallet.
- **Circular saw:** circular-bladed power saw, useful for cutting wood in all directions.
- **Electric jigsaw:** a small, powered blade supported at one end. Primarily designed for cutting curves in wood, metal and plastic.

▲ *When calculating how many tiles to order, remember to allow for the fact that you will probably be cutting a lot of tiles at the walls and along any diagonal edges. Generally, some of the offcuts can be used elsewhere, which minimizes wastage – at the right-hand end of the diagonal strip here, for instance – but this should not be relied upon.*

Setting out tiles

It is essential to spend a little care and time on setting things out before you start to tile a floor, whether with hard (see pages 40– 43) or flexible (see pages 48–51) materials, if you are to prevent problems. Tiles must not be allowed to go out of square, otherwise they will simply not fit together, and you must avoid ending up with an annoying little thin strip of tiles against the last wall.

▲ *Using tiles to reflect the other colours in an interior helps to create a sense of harmony and balance. Here the creamy floor tiles complement the soft pink tiles on the stairs to produce a warm effect, despite the cold, hard character of the raw materials and the predominance of straight edges. Muted colours can also help to create a sense of spaciousness.*

A regular room

Measure along the two opposite shortest walls to find the midpoint of each. Join these two marks together with a chalk line. Measure and mark 1m (39in) along this centre line on each side of the middle point. Measure 1m (39in) from the middle point at an estimated 90-degree angle. Measure the two diagonal lines between the marks on either side of the middle point and the 90-degree marks top and bottom, and adjust the latter's position until these two diagonals both measure 1.415m (55¾in).

You now have an angle of 90 degrees at the top and bottom. A straight line from these points to the middle of the centre line will meet the centre line at 90 degrees. The diagonals can serve as guide-lines for laying tiles diagonally at 45 degrees to the walls.

Use the chalk line to join the midpoint of the centre line with the 90-degree mark and extend this line across the full width of the room to mark the shorter centre line.

From these two lines, dry-lay a line of tiles up to each edge of the room to check that you will not be left with a thin strip of tiles at any point. If this happens, adjust the centre lines by half a tile's width to leave a decent border of tiles.

To ensure that all the tiles are laid without going out of square, it is best to divide up the entire floor into a series of boxes of approx 1 sq m (1 sq yd), starting from the two centre lines. The exact size of the 'boxes' will obviously be determined by the size of your chosen tiles.

When laying ceramic or quarry tiles remember to allow for the grout: about 6mm (¼in) for the smaller tiles and up to 10mm (⅜in) for larger, maybe slightly irregular handmade terracotta tiles. For example, you could lay thirty-six 15cm (6in) square tiles in a box measuring 936mm (36⅞in), or only nine 30cm (12in) square tiles in a box measuring 918mm (36⅛in). Remember to allow for an extra grout line around the edge of the room. Use the chalk line to mark out your boxes. Once you have marked out the floor with these guide-lines, you are ready to start tiling.

An irregular room

The principle for setting out an irregular room is the same as for a regular room

Setting out tiles

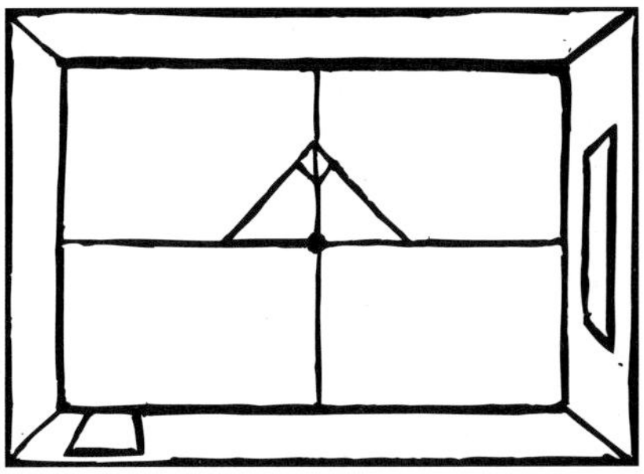

1 *Draw a line between the midpoints of the shortest walls; establish a right angle at the centre, as described.*

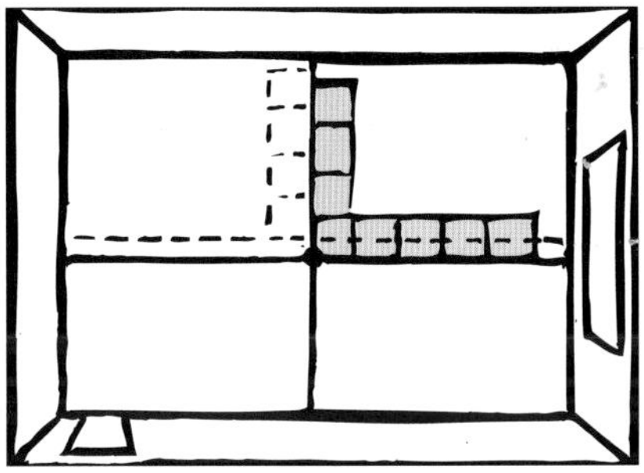

2 *Dry-lay tiles out from the centre to each wall. Adjust your centre if there is only a sliver of tile at any edge.*

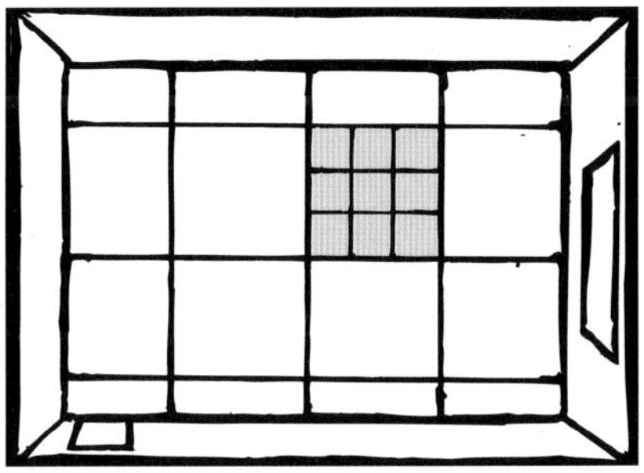

3 *Working from your centre point, mark out a grid over the whole floor area, to help you lay your tiles square.*

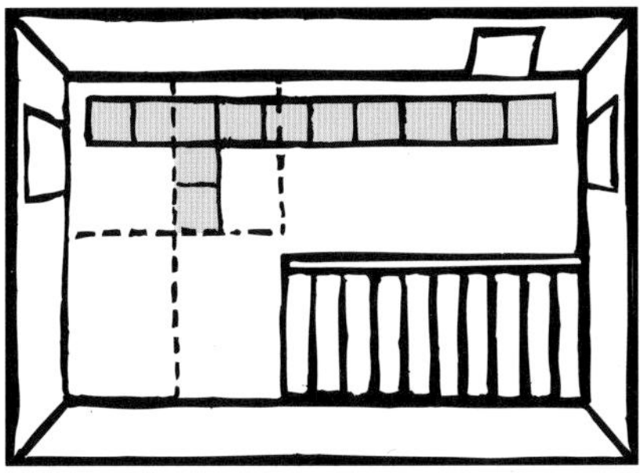

4 *In an irregularly shaped room adjust your centre point so that your tiles align with the longest wall.*

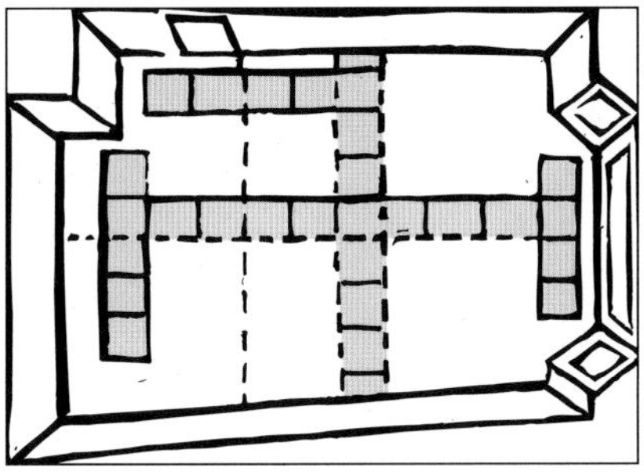

5 *In a room with lots of obstacles, lay your tiles square to a door; check for slivers and adjust your centre as usual.*

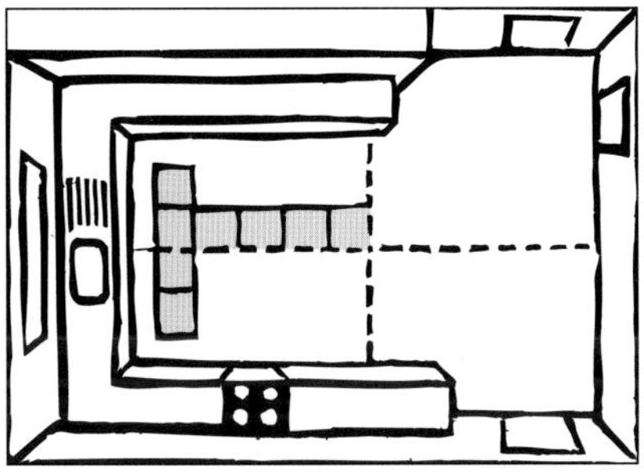

6 *You can adjust your centre lines to bisect a dominant feature – a range of units, for instance, or a bay window.*

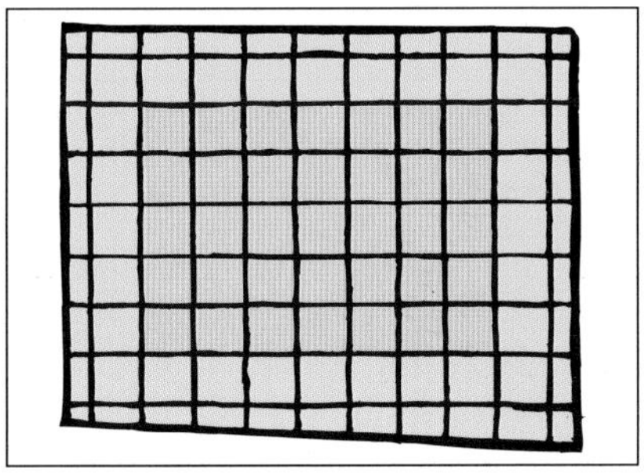

7 *To create a border, plan and lay a central area and then fill in the border, with cut tiles against the wall as usual.*

8 *A diagonally laid central area and straight border has the border laid first, followed by the diagonal panel.*

(above) except that you work from the longest and straightest wall. Adjust the position of the centre line so that a series of whole tiles can run from it to the longest wall. If the room is very out of square the final line of tiles – opposite the long, straight wall – will be cut at an angle and will vary considerably in their final size, but visually this is acceptable.

If the room is only slightly out of square, however, you may find that you end up with a thin sliver of tiles that gradually diminish as the room narrows. If this is the case, you should adjust the centre line by half a tile, so that you are basically working with half-tiles at the edge.

In rooms that are very irregular and have no obvious long wall, where to start to tile is really a matter of personal judgement. It is important to identify a feature in the room – the door, for instance – and align the tiles so that they run parallel to it.

If the room has a dominant feature, such as a range of kitchen units that are set out in a U-shape or a very large bay window, run the centre line through the 'U' to bisect it.

Provided the centre lines are at 90 degrees to each other, the tiles will always be square. Always dry-lay the tiles to check that there will be no fiddly bits, or make up a datum rod or tiling gauge (a length of wood with the tile, and grout if appropriate, intervals marked along its length) to save having to lay out the tiles repeatedly.

Setting out with a border

It is necessary to measure from the walls to establish the grid, but adjust the final position of the grid so that there is space for a border all the way around the room.

Either adjust the grid so that there are whole tiles lying against the border on two of the walls, or centre the grid right in the middle of the room and cut all the tiles against the border all the way around the room, provided the cut tiles do not end up being too narrow.

Tile the central area first and finish by tiling the border. Tiles that are laid diagonally should be finished with a border that runs parallel to the walls.

Hard flooring

As their survival in the oldest of our buildings testifies, the most enduring and practical of flooring materials are natural stone and tiles. Stone, marble and slate were once the only hard-wearing flooring materials available and were commonplace on the ground floors of cottages and cowsheds alike, wood being reserved for the gentler life on the upper levels once these were introduced. Tiles have been used since ancient times for the same reasons, but additionally they offer greater decorative possibilities.

▲ *As their shape and texture vividly illustrate, these ancient flagstones have almost certainly been in place for generations. Expensive to lay new today, this is the sort of flooring material we associate with unspoilt country cottages, although flagstones would once have been commonplace in a wider range of houses.*

Indeed, our knowledge of the Roman Empire is derived in part from the patterns and scenes depicted on the mosaic floors of the period, often the only remains of a building and its contents.

Today we have an ever-increasing choice of hard-flooring materials with which to furnish our homes (see pages 42–43). Exotic multicoloured slates and marbles are brought from all over the world, as are dozens of styles of beautiful and vividly coloured ceramic tiles. Even simple terracotta, always a popular choice, is now available in many different shades, shapes and sizes (see pages 42–43); the handmade tiles in subtly varying colours are the best.

The way in which a seemingly straightforward material is manufactured or prepared makes an enormous difference to the atmosphere that it helps to create. The textured surface of riven slate flagstones, for instance, is naturally at home in a simple country room that has been decorated in a traditional style; however the same material can equally be the perfect partner to, say, chrome and modern fittings if used in a contemporary bathroom but first cut into regular squares and honed smooth.

◀ *Hard flooring is an ever-popular and practical choice for transitional areas like hallways, because it is so practical. Slate tiles here have been laid on the diagonal, which always lends a certain elegance; and the alternation of light and dark tiles made from the same material is both subtle and decorative.*

▲ *Brightly coloured and patterned encaustic tiles provide a visual splash at the right-hand end of the bathroom and contrast strongly with the plain tiles used under the bath and to the left. Interestingly, the pattern painted on the bottom half of the door has been copied from one of the tiles in the patchwork arrangement on the floor.*

Fairly expensive and very durable, tiles and stone floors are a long-term investment and care should be given to the choices to be made. Hard floors are the preferred choice of those who live in warmer climates for practical reasons as indoors they create a cool refuge from the hot sun, both physically and psychologically. In many countries nearly all interior floors are tiled, with rugs being used to provide decorative relief and to help engender a sense of warmth and luxury.

For those of us who inhabit the cooler regions of the northern hemisphere, warmth is at a premium. In the kitchen and bathroom, however, where tough practicality is just as important, tiles and stone are still ideal. They are both waterproof and virtually indestructible, although dropping china or glass onto tiles or stone will result in a breakage.

Hallways, too, are a perfect environment for hard materials; stone's austere luxury will cause visitors to pause just briefly enough to reflect upon the initial impression it creates. In rooms that combine function with relaxation, such as a kitchen with a dining or seating area, two different materials can be used to demarcate the spaces. Tiles can be used for the kitchen floor, for instance, and wood for the living area. The wood is gentle and welcoming, the tiles provide practicality, and the two materials work well together.

Tone and colour are also important criteria. Brightly coloured tiles can be used as a dominant feature or neutral ones as a backdrop for brighter walls and fabrics or rugs: a cool slate floor simply decorated with a Persian rug in warm reds and blues is an especially rich combination.

Tiles are the perfect material for incorporating borders. Most manufacturers produce a range of complementary border tiles but it is possible to use any tiles as such, providing they fit together. For those with patience, mosaic offers interesting design potential, although it is probably wiser to use it in smaller rooms, and to stick to designs that do not use too many colours. Always use tiles made especially for floors, such as terracotta floor tiles; they are thicker than wall tiles which, being thin, might break.

Directory of hard floorings

Of all the exciting hard-flooring materials on offer, the most commonly used in the modern home are tiles. Due to a range of manufacturing processes floor tiles offer a wide choice of practical hard-wearing products suitable for most domestic situations. Ranging from natural earthy shades to bright and vibrant colours, they can also be chosen to complement any decor. Terracotta, the simplest and one of the oldest types, remains a time-honoured favourite for kitchens. Quarry tiles, which are at once economical and hard-wearing, are also enduringly popular. Ceramic floor tiles, available in many colours and styles, are perhaps the most versatile. And mosaic, used for centuries to decorate floors, is the perfect material for recreating a design, although simple, coloured borders set against a plain background are the easiest designs with which to work.

In addition, floor bricks can be used to create regular patterns, and stone, whether it be natural or reconstructed, can provide just the right touch for some interiors. Slate, for instance, is a very practical material and comparatively easy to lay because it is so thin; some sheets are hardly thicker than a ceramic tile. Finally, while metal flooring may not be a viable option for most people, it is the ideal material if the ultimate in industrial chic is required.

Terracotta tiles

Unglazed and softer than other types of tile, terracotta is made from extruded or hand-formed clay. It is available in a number of shapes and sizes, from small hexagons to large squares. The colours range from dusky ochres to oranges through to reds. Part of the charm of terracotta is precisely this colour variation, within each tile and from tile to tile, as well as the textural variations of the surface. These porous tiles must be finished with linseed oil and waxed for protection.

Quarry tiles

Quarry tiles are made from extruded or hand-formed clay which is fired at higher temperatures than terracotta to vitrify it, a process that gives the tiles their durability and makes them very hard-wearing and waterproof. The colour range is a little limited; buffs, reds and browns are the dominant tones although white and black tiles have been produced. The tiles usually have a dull satin finish. Variously sized square or rectangular quarry tiles are available – and some 'key squares' too (see pages 46–47). 1

Ceramic tiles

Ceramic floor tiles are made from a dust-pressed clay that is fired at high temperatures. Fully vitrifed ceramic tiles are the most waterproof of all

tiles, making them suitable for the wettest areas – such as bathrooms. Ceramic floor tiles are not glazed; glazed tiles are normally too slippery unless the glaze has a roughened surface. They may have decorative patterns or little studs on the surface for textural variation and slip resistance. Oxides, added during the manufacturing process, give these tiles the widest range of colours of any unglazed tile – including plain white. Ceramic tiles are thinner than quarry or terracotta tiles and their uniform thickness enables trouble-free installation. They can, however, be polished for a more glamorous look.

Mosaic tiles

Mosaic tiles are tiny, cut from glass, coloured ceramic, terracotta, stone or marble and fixed to a backing sheet for speedy installation. Their appearance varies both according to the material and to whether it has been machine- or hand-cut. 2

Encaustic tiles

Encaustic tiles are either plain-coloured or have a decorative pattern applied to their surface which has a soft, matt quality with colours that blend into each other. A design is painted onto a mould using natural oxides and then a plain tile is pressed into the design to transfer the design onto the tile's surface. 4

Brick

The bricks that are used for decorative floors are much the same as terracotta tiles. They are, however, thicker, and they do require a solid base. Because of their small, regular size, bricks are perfect for creating patterns: herringbone is traditional but something more individual works equally well.

Limestone

A sedimentary rock formed from coral and shell deposits at the bottom of warm seas, limestone has a considerably varied character which ranges

4

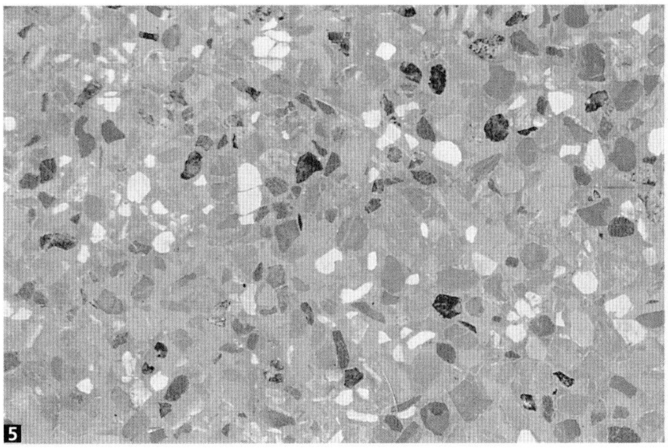

5

from almost white and fine-grained through a coarser texture with embedded fossils to very dark greens and blues. It can be finished in a variety of ways, from a rough to highly polished surface. As it is very porous and stains easily it should always be sealed. Antique limestone is sourced from a number of historical sites, but these cannot last for ever. New limestone is more regular and lacks the distressed quality of well-worn limestone – although some suppliers have tried to recreate examples with an aged look.

Slate

A metamorphic rock formed from mudstones and shales, slate splits neatly into thin sheets. Riven slate has a naturalistic, rough and uneven appearance. Typically it is cut into squares or chopped, which gives the edges a complementary rougher look. Slate is usually blue-grey with a silvery quality, although there are some extraordinary colours available too, ranging from pale parchment with warm buff highlights to dark reds and rusts. As slate is so varied it can be used successfully anywhere that calls for a hard-wearing and practical surface.

Sandstone

Sandstone is a sedimentary stone, formed from the grains of igneous rocks. It can be found in colours that range from a soft cream to ochre and warm brick red. As it is hard-wearing, it has come to be associated with flagstones, most popularly York stone. It is particularly useful in situations where slip resistance is important – in shower rooms, for instance, although it may be too rough for some feet. Its gritty surface can make it difficult to clean too, which also makes it less than ideal for kitchens. 3

Marble

Metamorphosed limestone, marble is characterized by coloured mineral veins which run through it. It is extremely diverse: for example, Carrara marble is a soft grey interspersed with a blurry, indistinct black veining that is quietly elegant, whereas Brochella marbles are vivid reds and blacks, with colourful swirling veins, perfect for proclaiming wealth and power.

Terrazzo

This is a material manufactured from marble chips bound together with a cement-based adhesive. It is made into slabs or tiles and polished to a high sheen. The colour is dependent on the type of marble used. Different colours can be incorporated into one slab to create patterned borders and centres that simply fit together to complete a repeating or symmetrical design. Traditionally found around the Mediterranean, terrazzo is an extremely hard-wearing material often used in commercial environments. 5

Quartzite

One of the hardest natural stone flooring materials, quartzite comes in a wide range of plain and variegated colours from soft greys to warmer buffs, as well as much darker colours such as sombre greens and near-black. Quartzite has a riven, slip-resistant surface which, together with its durability, makes it a popular choice for commercial applications.

Metal flooring

The ubiquitous aluminium treadplate is found everywhere nowadays: from the backs of lorries to warehouses. It is available in 2.44 x 1.22m (8 x 4ft) sheets and is easy to lay over an existing floor either as large sheets or cut into tiles. Aluminium treadplate is slip-resistant and non-corrosive. The gleaming surface perfectly complements a contemporary interior.

Laying ceramic tiles

▲ *Machine-made ceramic tiles always look smarter if tile spacers are used when the tiles are set into the adhesive, to ensure that joints are evenly spaced and neat. This type of tile is easy to cut cleanly, which is a useful characteristic if a lot of cuts need to be made – around obstructions, for example, or if the tiles are laid on the diagonal.*

Modern ceramic floor tiles are regularly shaped and quite thin, making them easier to cut than other types of tile. If you are laying the tiles on a timber floor, prime the floor first with either a general builder's PVA adhesive or a special tile primer for wood floors. If the floor is at all uneven or insufficiently rigid, first cover it with plywood or WBP (Weather and Boil Proof) chipboard (see pages 34–35).

Laying the tiles

Begin by setting out and drawing up a grid of 'boxes' across the floor (see pages 38–39). Mix up the tile adhesive according to the manufacturer's instructions, adding any special additives for greater flexibility if you are covering a wood floor. Tile adhesive has a limited pot life, about 20 minutes, so do not mix up more than you will realistically be able to use in the time available.

Lay your first tile in the corner furthest from the door. In order accurately to position this tile, dry-lay a line of tiles from the centre point to the far wall along the centre line, and then draw a line at right angles to the centre line along the far edge of the last whole tile. Dry-lay tiles along the new line and, in the same way as before, draw a line on the far side of your last whole tile at right angles to your guideline. Providing this line is parallel to the centre line the last tile you dry-laid is your 'first tile'. Only spread the adhesive over an area of approx. 1sq m (1sq yd) at a time. Using the recommended side of a notched spreader or trowel, apply the adhesive to the correct depth, normally approx. 3mm (⅛in). Depending on the adhesive being used, it may be necessary to butter the back of the tile with adhesive as well. Press the tile into position with a slight twisting motion; it is important to bed the tile into the adhesive without any air gaps. For neat and even joints, usually 6–12mm (¼–½in), use plastic spacers between the tiles. Continue laying the tiles in the first marked square, checking the tiles are level with a spirit level and straight edge. You need to work fast, as you have a very limited amount of time to reposition any tiles that are incorrectly laid. If any adhesive gets on the surface of a tile clean it off immediately with a damp cloth; ensure too that the joints are adhesive-free.

When the first grid box has been laid, apply adhesive to the second and continue laying tiles along the far wall. Then complete the second row of squares and continue laying the tiles in rows of boxes, working back towards the door. Allow the tile

▲ *Wide joints look particularly effective when used between small tiles. They are also helpful if the tiles are not all the same size: different-sized gaps are less noticeable than different-sized tiles. Two widths of joint have been used here deliberately, adding to the charm of this arrangement of handmade and painted tiles.*

adhesive to dry thoroughly before walking on the tiles. Conventional adhesives usually need at least 24 hours although fast-setting adhesives can take only a few hours.

It will probably be necessary to cut tiles around the edges of the room to fit; if you lay the tiles on the diagonal, you will need to cut at least one in every two tiles. Ceramic tiles can be cut using a tile-cutting jig.

To determine where to cut a border tile place a whole tile over the last laid whole tile. To allow for the grout, place a tile on its side between this tile and the wall and place another tile up against it. Mark the middle tile with a soft pencil where the tile above it ends. Place the tile in the jig and cut along the marked line. Butter the back of the cut tile and press into position. Continue until all the border tiles have been laid, leaving the four corners until last in order to cut them accurately.

Where a tile has to go around an architrave, use a tile nibbler to chip away the edge of a tile. For pipes, the tile will have to be cut in half and a semi-circle nibbled out of each half to take the pipe; or you could cut a notch into one edge. When laying the two halves, leave only a thin joint between them so the cut is less noticeable when grouted.

Grouting the tiles

When all the tiles have been laid and the adhesive is dry, fill the tile joints with a tile grout suitable for floors. Conventional grout is a powder mixed with water according to the manufacturer's instructions. It is available in colours ranging from off-white to dark grey. For tiles laid over wood floors, remember to mix in a flexible additive.

For food-preparation areas an epoxy grout is a good idea because it is extremely hard and easily cleaned. Epoxy grout consists of two components that are mixed together, and then a powder filler is added to bulk it out. Always follow the manufacturer's instructions. Pour the grout onto the surface and spread it into the joints with the aid of a rubber squeegee, working on small areas at a time. After 15 minutes, clean any excess grout off the surface with a damp cloth. Once the grout has hardened sufficiently, polish the tiles with a clean, dry cloth.

Laying ceramic tiles

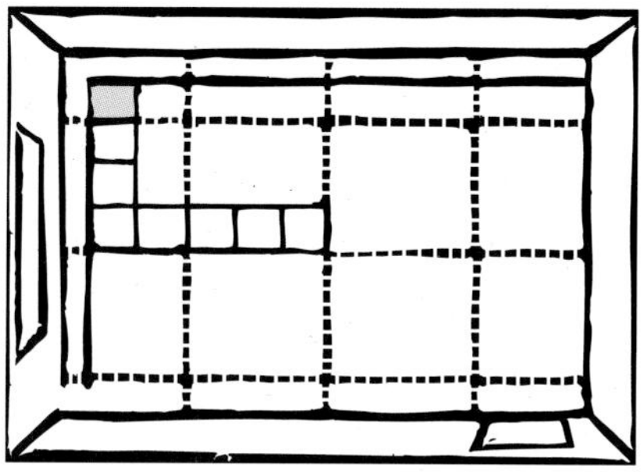

***1** Lay your first tile in the furthest corner: dry-lay two lines of tiles from the centre to find the correct position.*

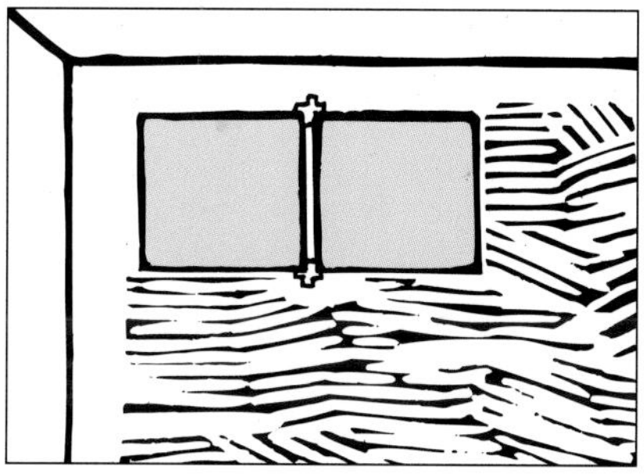

***2** Spread adhesive over a manageable area and press the tiles into position; use plastic spacers for even joints.*

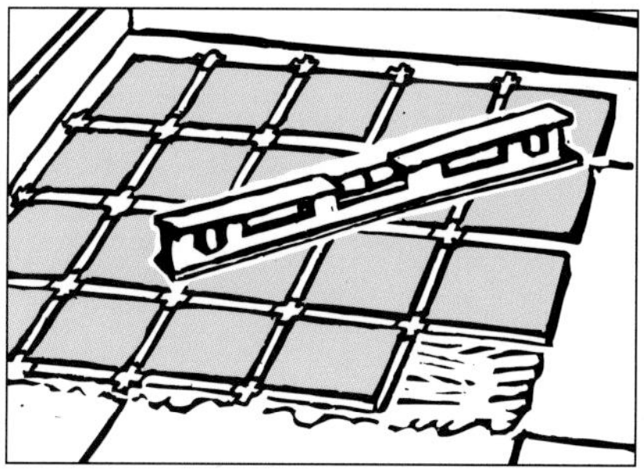

***3** Working fast, continue to lay tiles to complete the first marked square, checking frequently that they are level.*

***4** Cut border tiles accurately using the simple method described, remembering to allow for grout at the edge.*

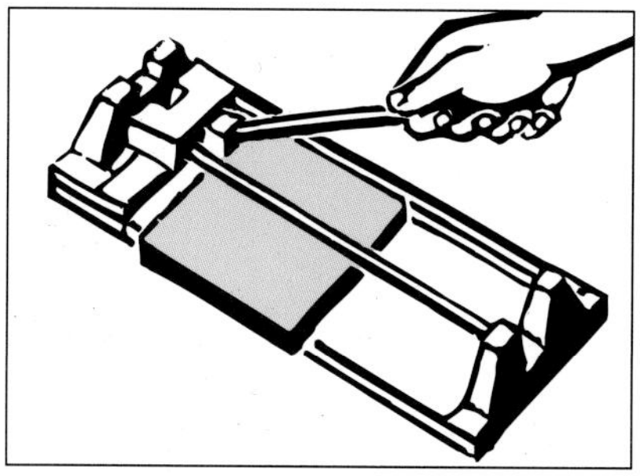

***5** To cut all the border tiles effortlessly and efficiently, place the marked tile in a jig and press the lever to cut.*

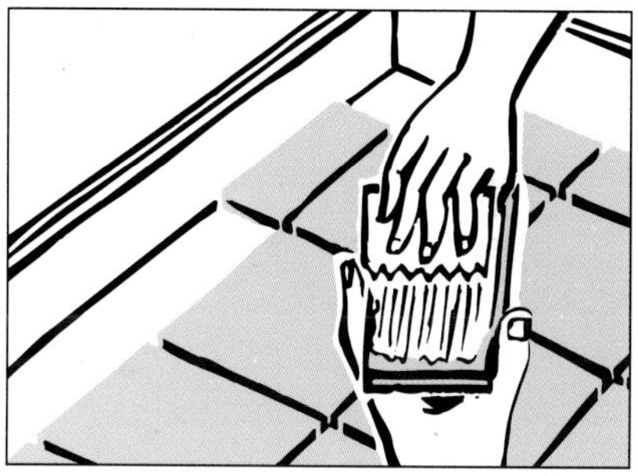

***6** The cut border tiles will need to be 'buttered' with adhesive before being pressed into position.*

***7** When the adhesive is dry, pour grout onto the surface. Spread it into the joints a small area at a time.*

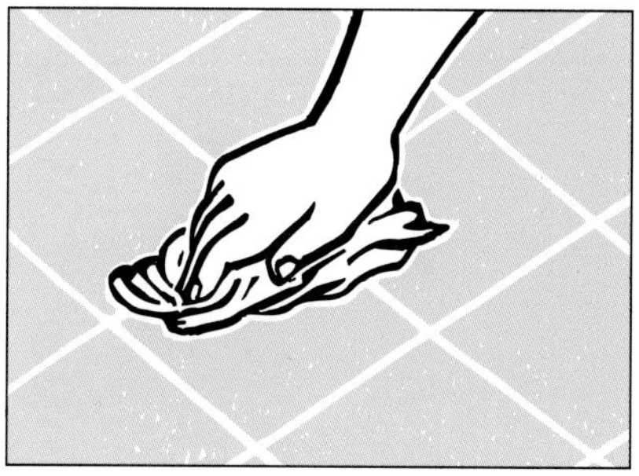

***8** Any excess grout should be cleaned from the surface with a damp cloth, before it is polished.*

Laying terracotta tiles

Larger and heavier than ceramic tiles, terracotta tiles need a thicker adhesive bed, especially if the tiles are handmade and vary in thickness, or if they have bowed during manufacture. The method described here can be used for other types of tile such as quarry or slate, the thick adhesive bed being used to absorb any difference in tile thickness. Although a sand-and-cement mix can be used for many heavy tiles, it is not really suitable for terracotta tiles. Because they are very porous, they may react with the cement to cause efflorescence – when the soluble salts come to the surface as a white stain. Use a thick-bed adhesive, which can be applied at any thickness from 5mm to 2.5cm (¼ to 1in). Thick-bed adhesive can happily be used on an uneven floor base and dries very quickly, in some cases enabling tiling and grouting to be carried out in the same day. Very uneven surfaces, however, should be prepared as described on pages 34–35.

The principles for marking out and laying the tiles are much the same as for laying ceramic tiles (see pages 44–45). You start in the furthest corner, having located the centre point and adjusted it, and having marked up a grid which will help to keep you straight. Mix up the tile adhesive according to the manufacturer's instructions. Some types of thick-bed adhesive are simply poured onto the floor and spread out to an even level with an appropriate type of spreader, and then the tiles are laid straight onto it. Other types of adhesive require the back of the tile to be buttered with adhesive as well: always follow the manufacturer's directions. Handmade tiles may vary slightly in size and thickness, so apply more adhesive to the backs of the thinner tiles and allow a wide gap, approx. 12mm (½in), between the tiles; any variations in size will be taken up within the joints. It is important to keep an eye on the marked-out grid to ensure the tiles are laid square and to keep checking the tiles are level with the spirit level and straight edge. Once the central area of the floor is finished, fill in the border – i.e., lay all the whole tiles you can before cutting your border and corner tiles.

Cutting tiles

The easiest way to cut terracotta tiles is with an angle grinder fitted with a stone-cutting wheel. Cut a groove into the tile to two thirds of the tile's depth and then snap it in two. The cutter will, if required, cut or grind through the whole thickness of the tile –useful for cutting awkward shapes out of a tile to go round pipes and other obstructions.

▶ Rectangular quarry tiles have been laid in a staggered pattern like bricks in this high-ceilinged, cool white sitting room. Great care must be taken to avoid letting the tiles go out of line. These particular tiles are richly variegated which creates decorative interest on the floor without the need for any major planning effort.

▲ Old, handmade tiles look very effective in this kitchen; they can be very tricky to lay, however, compared to machine-made tiles. Remember that the joints between handmade tiles must vary in width in order to allow for slight variations in tile size, and bear in mind that handmade tiles can vary in thickness too.

Laying terracotta tiles

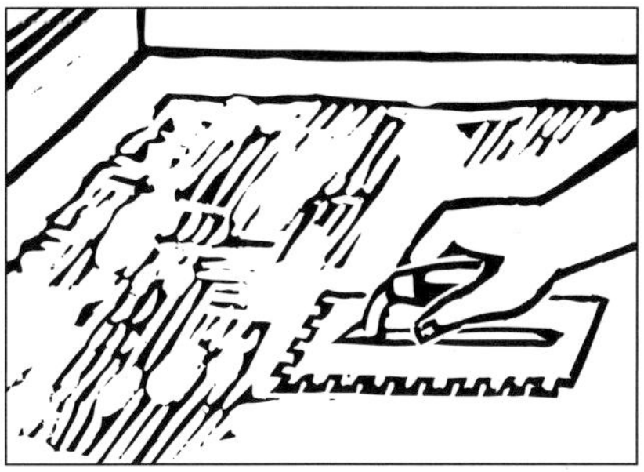

1 Spread adhesive over approx. 1sq m (1sq yd) to a depth specified by the manufacturer, using a notched trowel.

2 Some adhesives require the back of the tile to be 'buttered' as well, to make both contact surfaces tacky.

3 Using a spirit level, check regularly that the tiles you have laid are level, and certainly after each grid box.

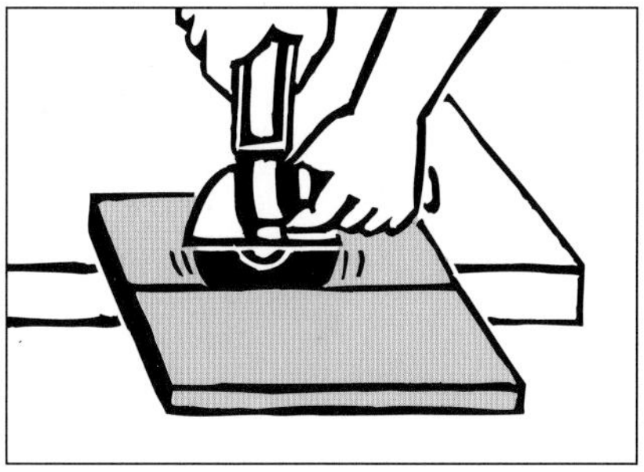

4 It may be possible to cut some tiles with a jig but most will need the power of an angle grinder.

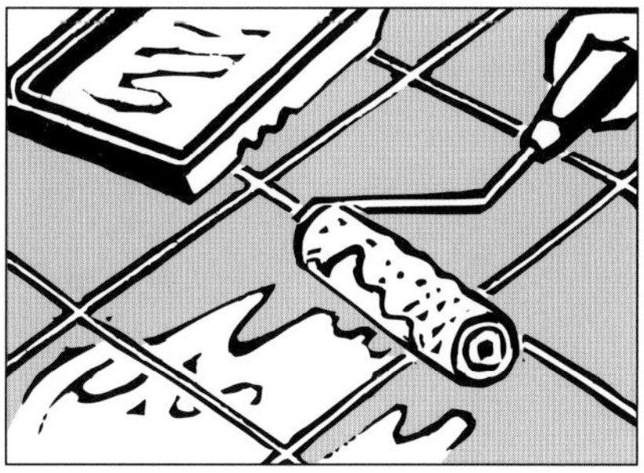

5 Terracotta tiles will need to be sealed with a coat of boiled linseed oil before they are grouted.

6 Grout the joints of porous tiles with a pointing trowel: fill the joints and avoid spilling grout on the surface.

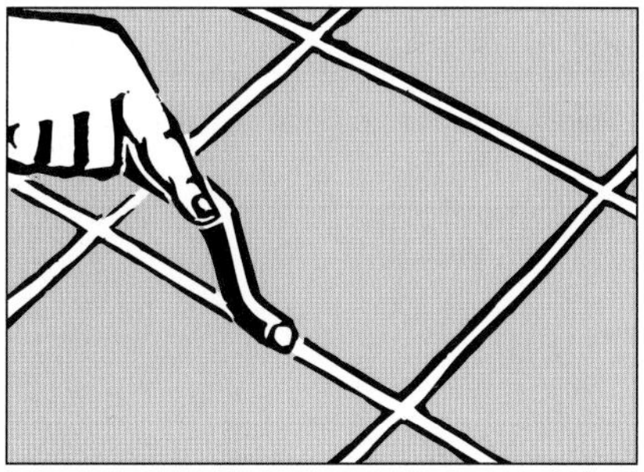

7 Push grout well down into all the joints – to support the edges fully. Use a metal pipe to create a concave finish.

8 Apply wax with a cloth after a secondary coat of sealer, and when dry, polish it off with a rotary floor machine.

Sealing

Terracotta and quarry tiles are very porous and must be sealed before you add grouting in order to provide a hard-wearing and easy-to-clean surface. Ensure the surfaces of the tiles are free from dust and any traces of tile adhesive. Brush one coat of boiled linseed oil over the tiles with a brush or short-haired paint roller. It is important to apply an even coat to avoid the risk of streaking. The oil will soak into the tile, the surface losing its gloss 2–10 minutes after application. If it appears matt in less time than that, apply the oil more liberally. Allow the sealer to dry and then grout. A second coat of sealer should be applied after grouting.

Grouting

Grout terracotta tiles with a grout that is suitable for wide joints; porous tiles are grouted using a pointing method rather than by simply spreading the grout over the surface as you would for ceramic tiles. Fill the joints using a pointing trowel, and avoid spilling any of the grout onto the surface of the tiles. Finish the grout by making it slightly concave; bend a round metal pipe into a convenient shape and use that.

Some types of handmade tiles benefit from 'slurry grouting', a technique which fills in all the pits and dents to create an antiqued appearance. Mix up the grout to a creamy consistency and grout as you would ceramic tiles (see pages 44–45), ensuring that the grout fills all the crevices. Clean the excess grout off the surface with a damp sponge.

Finishing off

Apply a second coat of seal once the grout has thoroughly dried, using the oil more sparingly than before as the tiles will be less porous. Any excess oil that does not soak in after 20 minutes should be cleaned from the surface of the tile. After the oil has had time to soak into the tiles fully, which usually takes a few hours or overnight, the tiles can be waxed. Use a proprietary floor wax and wax the floor twice. The new floor should then be waxed once a week for the following month in order to build up a smooth and hard-wearing, yet mellow surface.

Flexible flooring

Probably used in more environments than any other type of floor-covering and usually overlooked, flexible materials are the unsung heroes of the flooring world. Consisting of just a thin layer, only a few millimetres (fractions of an inch) thick, they add colour and texture to any floor, transforming it at a stroke. Their tough practicality, economy and easy maintenance ensure their presence in locations from the kitchen to the factory floor and they are ubiquitous in hospitals, airports and factories.

Although they are usually laid in the more demanding areas of the home – the kitchen and bathroom – flexible materials can be used in any room and would be a particularly sensible choice for a hallway. In practice, these materials should never wear out in a domestic situation.

Linoleum, the forerunner of more modern materials such as vinyl, was once all that many people could afford to lay over their floorboards to increase their practicality while at the same time enhancing their appearance. In its most usual manifestation, a dreary brown colour, it was used in many public buildings. Linoleum virtually disappeared as domestic flooring with the introduction of the more versatile PVC flooring known as vinyl, but having only recently shed its traditionally dowdy image, it is currently undergoing a real renaissance. It has brightened up considerably and now offers a dazzling array of bright and cheery colours that look bang up to date.

Due to its ready availability and particularly extensive potential for decoration, vinyl has been the flooring material of choice for many years. It is possible to add far more colour and design to the surface of vinyl than of linoleum and consequently it is made in a wide range of patterned, flecked and marbled hues, as well as in imitation of expensive natural flooring materials. In some cases it is hard to tell apart from the real thing. Indeed, it can be even more expensive to buy than the real thing, the vinyl version often being chosen because of its low maintenance and because it is warmer and softer than its natural counterparts, such as stone.

Rubber, another material that has recently increased in popularity as a domestic floorcovering, is extremely durable. It recovers from minor surface nicks and resists burns, so it continues to look good for longer than other flexible flooring products. The raised and studded non-slip surface of rubber makes it an appealing material.

Cork has, in the past, been a very popular natural product, although in recent years it has gone slightly out of favour. In the right setting, however, it can still prove extremely practical. Available in a small range of natural colours, it is a very attractive choice, and worth considering for any budget-conscious scheme with a bias towards the environment.

Flexible flooring materials are available in either sheet or tile form and are so thin that they never cause problems with raised thresholds. As sheet floorings can be tricky to install, it may be worth having more expensive material laid professionally. A large sheet is heavy and awkward and can be difficult to manoeuvre in a room. And just one small slip of the knife can spoil what would otherwise be a perfect finish. Linoleum also contracts and expands unpredictably, which can make it difficult to fit. Vinyl is easier to lay than other sheet materials (see pages 52–55).

Tiles are among the easiest flexible products for the amateur to lay at home. They are also easier to use creatively than the sheet equivalent: installing borders or key squares, for example, is a comparatively straightforward matter (see pages 56–57). Vinyl and linoleum can both be cut and inlaid with different-coloured pieces of the same type of material. With linoleum this can either be done when the floor is laid or later, when you want to brighten it up, when you can inlay shapes. Some vinyl manufacturers provide a very comprehensive range of designs for inlaying, either off the shelf or to special commission.

It is possible to create complex borders and designs for vinyl and linoleum using sophisticated cutting technology but the more intricate designs do require professional installation by highly skilled practitioners.

◄◄ Modern linoleum is not only supremely practical but is now available in an excellent range of contemporary colours. It can be inlaid to create very intricate designs: indeed, an extravagant abstract inlaid design in watery blues and greys provides the main point of visual interest in this plain white panelled bathroom.

◄ Cork is a very practical material; its natural golden colour will warm any room – both decoratively and physically. The raw material usually appears on the market as tiles; these can be made of granulated cork, or designed to form simple patterns within a tile format, as illustrated in this kitchen.

Directory of flexible floor-coverings

All the various types of flexible flooring are hard-wearing. Quality varies from product to product within each category and prices vary considerably, particularly amongst vinyls, ranging from fairly reasonable to very expensive. Flexible flooring materials are either sold as tiles which can be laid in patterns, or in sheet form that is available in various widths up to about 4m (13ft). Once a decision has been made regarding type, choosing a particular colour or pattern will obviously be the next hurdle, and the potential for having fun is huge, so versatile is the modern raw material.

1

2

Linoleum

A completely natural product with excellent environmental credentials, linoleum is made from linseed oil, organic fillers, such as wood flour, and minerals such as chalk and coloured pigment. The ingredients are mixed into a paste, rolled into sheets with a hessian or fibreglass backing and then baked for three weeks. The result is a hard material with a slight sheen. Linoleum is available in a comprehensive range of hues, either plain or marbled with additional colour. Plain, coloured linoleum has a rather dead quality that shows marks easily, and should only be used if a very unobtrusive floor colour is required. Being naturally anti-static and antibacterial, linoleum is ideal for industrial and hospital applications.

Linoleum is very versatile. It can be inlaid with other colours, offering infinite design permutations. **1**

Vinyl

Made from PVC (polyvinyl chloride), vinyl is a tough and flexible plastic material. It is available in various thicknesses depending on the type of environment in which it is to be used. The simplest vinyls are made from a single thickness of coloured vinyl that is then marbled or flecked with streaks of a secondary colour; alternatively, several different colours can be blended together. More elaborate vinyls are made in layers, a plain backing with a patterned layer fixed over it. The top layer can be clear while coloured flecks are embedded over a different base to give a subtle three-dimensional look; these silicon carbide flecks give the material excellent anti-slip properties and also a glittery appearance. The most sophisticated designs are made by sandwiching a printed sheet between the backing and a clear facing. This printed sheet often carries images of natural materials which, depending on the quality, can be startlingly realistic or an obviously faked pastiche. The surface of vinyl is usually smooth, although it can be textured for greater slip resistance or better to imitate the texture of natural materials. The wear layer is often treated in order to make it very low-maintenance as a floor-covering, or even harder-wearing.

4

3

Vinyl can also be inlaid. Many domestic vinyls have a cushioned back for a softer and more comfortable feel. 4

Rubber

Rubber flooring is made from both synthetic and natural materials with mineral fillers and pigments added for colour and body. It is so flexible that it can take sharp knocks and cigarette burns without sustaining serious damage; thus it is used in situations where an extremely hard-wearing surface is required. The surface can be either smooth, or studded or ribbed, which, although mainly intended for slip resistance, gives the material a unique decorative quality that is part of its appeal. It has a slightly softer, more substantial quality than vinyl and provides a practical surface that is easily cleaned. It is also very stable, which means it will not shrink or deteriorate significantly over time, and is available in a range of plain colours as well as marbled and granular styles. 2

Cork

Cork is a natural product derived from the bark of the cork oak tree; once the bark is gathered, the tree will grow a new bark which will be ready to harvest again nine years later.

Cork has many practical advantages over some of the other flooring materials. It is durable and can be very economical to lay. It is an excellent insulator so it always feels warm to the touch. And it is a good sound barrier; indeed, cork can be laid as an underlay for other types of flooring to provide greater sound insulation. It is available in sheets or, more commonly, as tiles of various thicknesses.

Cork tiles can either be made from strips of cork veneer fixed over a compressed cork backing or be simply granulated and pressed together with an adhesive which gives the product a speckled appearance; different-sized granules produce different surface textures. Naturally brown in colour, cork is available in a limited colour range. Tiles of different hues can be combined, thereby offering some design flexibility. Tiles that are not adhesive-backed are stuck down onto the floor using applied adhesive.

Cork tiles are supplied either pre-finished with a varnish or plain, in which case they will need to be sealed after installation. Some tiles are sold laminated and are particularly hard-wearing and maintenance-free. Laying unfinished tiles, on the other hand, can present problems because the material is prone to bubbling. If you decide to use cork tiles in a potentially wet environment, it is a good idea to give the tiles an extra coat of varnish once they have been laid, to fill any small gaps between tiles and making the whole floor more waterproof. 3

Laying sheet vinyl

▲ *It is preferable to lay sheet vinyl in one piece, not only because it is less prone to damage than strips, but also because it looks neater. Seams between strips would spoil the clean lines of this room. It is surprising and interesting to note how well this modern grey vinyl sits with old wooden panelling and antique chairs.*

Ideally, sheet vinyl should be laid in one piece so as to minimize the number of seams. These not only look unattractive but also allow the ingress of dirt and moisture that can cause problems in the future. Most sheet vinyls are available in widths of up to 4m (13ft), so only the widest of rooms should require a seam. It is much easier to lay vinyl in an empty room, before kitchen units, for example, or bathroom fittings are installed; the fewer the obstructions requiring fiddly cutting the more likely it is that the end result will have a professional look and be fully waterproof. If you need to remove the vinyl at a later date, just cut around the units or fittings placed over it with a trimming knife.

All sheet vinyl should be unwrapped loosely and left in the room in which it is to be laid for at least 24 hours before laying. This will give the material time to settle and acclimatize to the atmosphere before you start making cuts.

Fitting the vinyl

Cut the sheet of vinyl to size allowing 5cm (2in) extra on all edges. This can be done in a room larger than the one it will be fitted in; if there is not a sufficiently large room available cut the vinyl outside, making sure that it is kept clean. For vinyl that has to be fitted as two strips, unroll it and trim the ends only. It may be necessary to cut more off one end than the other in order to ensure that any pattern matches from one strip to the next.

Choose the longest and straightest wall to work from. Bring the sheet into the room and unroll it diagonally. Then shuffle the material around so it is square to the long wall with a 3cm (1¼in) gap between the edge of the vinyl and the long wall. The material should curve up the skirting boards or walls on the other edges of the room. Check the vinyl is square to the wall by measuring from the wall to the pattern at both ends of the room and adjust if required, and then push a soft broom over the vinyl to ensure that it is flat on the floor and that there are no air bubbles trapped underneath.

Scribing a line

To cut the vinyl to fit the long wall precisely, use a small block of wood pressed against the wall and overlapping the vinyl to first scribe a line. Slide the block along the wall from one end to the other, at the same time holding a marker pen against it with the tip pressing on the vinyl. The line should exactly follow the contours of the wall. Cut the vinyl along the marked line using a sharp trimming knife. If you are feeling confident, you can simply run the knife along with the block of wood (instead of the pen) to cut the vinyl directly. Push the cut edge against the wall; it should fit perfectly.

Cutting corners

To enable the vinyl to lie flat, make relief cuts at the corners. At external corners simply press the vinyl against the base of the skirting

Laying sheet vinyl

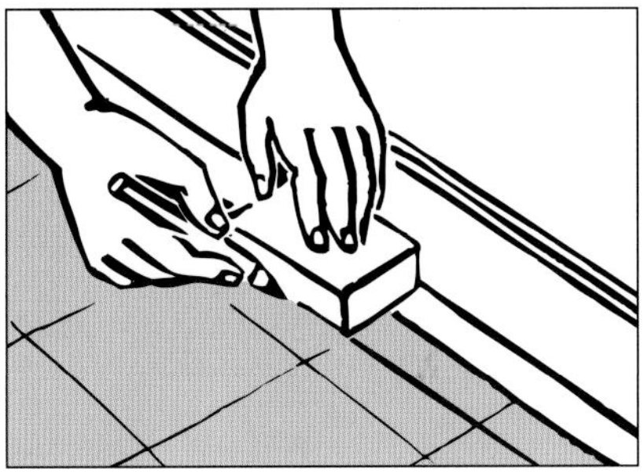

1 Using a block, scribe a line along the edge of the vinyl with a marker pen, following the contours of the wall.

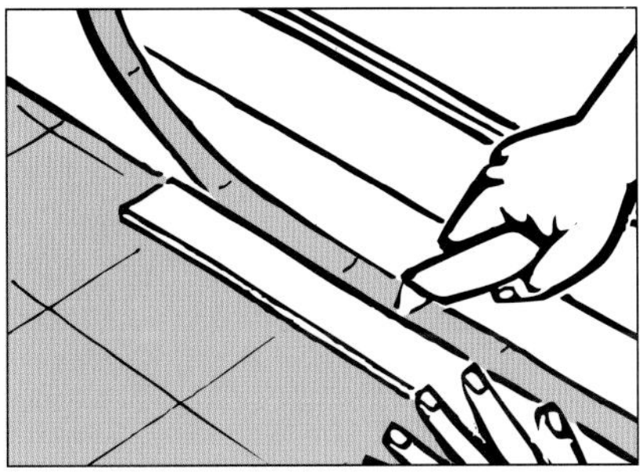

2 Cut the first edge of the vinyl to fit exactly by cutting along this marked line with a sharp craft knife.

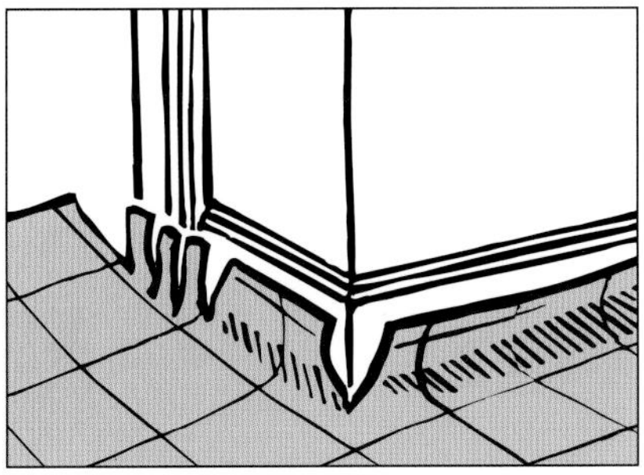

3 At external corners, press the vinyl into the base of the skirting board, and make a series of relief cuts.

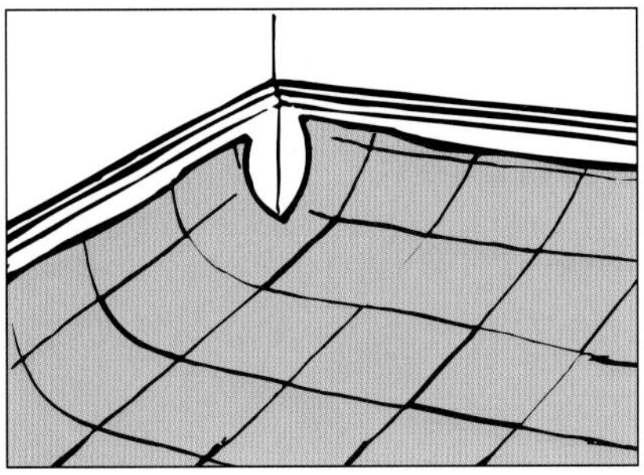

4 At internal corners, cut the corner off the vinyl as described at the measured point to let the vinyl lie flat.

5 Using a paint scraper, push the vinyl right into the base of the wall; create a series of flaps to aid neat trimming.

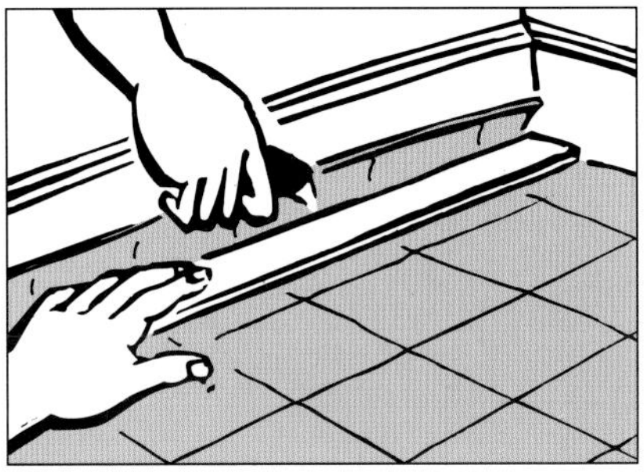

6 Alternatively, if you are confident, push the vinyl with a metal ruler and cut along its edge in one stroke.

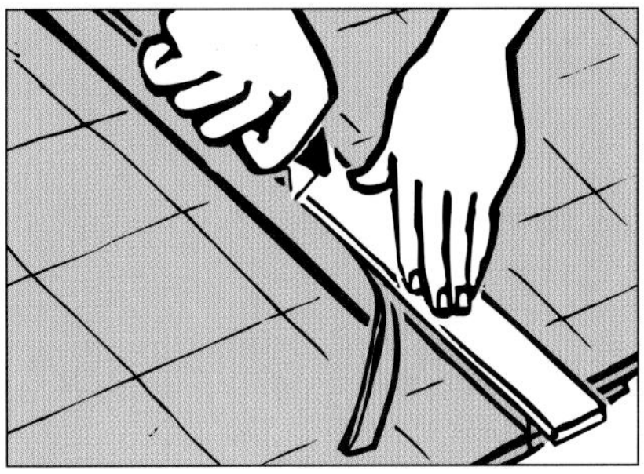

7 Cut through two overlapping pieces of vinyl to create an invisible seam, preferably along the line of a pattern.

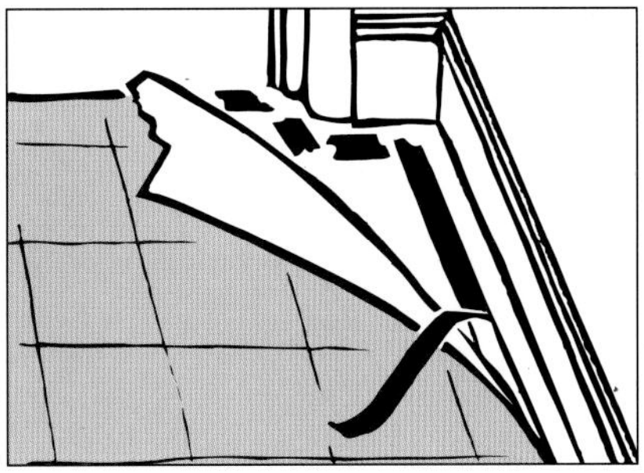

8 Secure the trimmed vinyl sheet at strategic points using special vinyl-to-floor double-sided tape.

board and cut up from that point to the edge of the vinyl so that the material lies flat. At internal corners cut off a triangle from the corner of the vinyl so that when the vinyl is folded up, the two flaps of excess material do not overlap. Do this by folding the vinyl back towards the centre of the room by about 5cm (2in) and measure from the corner to the fold. Measure from the fold towards the corner point of the vinyl by the same amount as the first measurement. Cut the corner off the vinyl at the measured point; the vinyl should now lie flat against the wall with neat flaps of excess material along the walls. Trim these by first pressing the vinyl into the base of the skirting board at intervals of 15cm (6in). Use a stiff paint scraper to push the material right into the angle between the skirting board and the wall. Cut along the fold and remove the piece. Repeat this process until you are left with a series of flaps. Pull the material away from the wall and place a straight edge along the base of the flaps, then trim them off so the vinyl fits neatly against the wall. If you are confident with the knife, cut along the edge of the vinyl in one stroke; use a metal edge when you would otherwise use a paint scraper, and cut.

Cutting seams

Where a seam is necessary, lay the second piece of vinyl over the first so that the pattern matches up. Lay a metal straight edge over the two pieces of vinyl where the seam is to be. Try to place the seam on the line of any pattern as the seam will be less noticeable there. Cut along the straight edge through both pieces of vinyl; the edges should fit perfectly together.

Fixing and gluing

Sheet vinyl sold for domestic use is usually the cushioned type that is used without an adhesive, although some gluing is necessary in certain areas: near doorways, around heavy objects that might be moved, dragging the vinyl with them, and on any seams. Use a special vinyl-to-floor double-sided tape or an acrylic vinyl floor adhesive to secure the floor-covering, following the manufacturer's instructions. ▷

Cutting around obstacles

The easiest way of cutting around obstacles such as a washbasin is to make a paper template. Lining paper is an excellent material for this. If necessary, stick several sheets together to make a sufficiently large sheet. Make a release cut in the paper so that you can position the paper around the obstacle with the cut side against the skirting board. Make a second release cut at 90 degrees to the first, and then continue to make a series of release cuts until the paper lies flat around the obstruction. Fold each flap of paper so that it creases into the corner between the floor and the obstacle. Mark the creases with a pencil line, lift the paper away, and cut along the lines to form the template.

Next you must loosely fit the vinyl in order to trim the edge at the skirting board. Make release cuts in the vinyl at 90 degrees from each other, just as in the initial stage of making the paper template. Position the vinyl around the obstacle and trim it all along the skirting. Then pull the vinyl away from the obstacle. Tape together the first release cut in the paper template so that the shape of the obstacle is clearly defined.

Position the template over the vinyl so that the edges of the paper and vinyl correspond and the release cuts in the vinyl match up with the edges of the hole in the paper. Mark and cut the hole out of the vinyl and then refit the vinyl into position.

Alternatively, adapt the method you employed to fit your vinyl flush to the first wall (see pages 52–53). Use a block of wood as an amateur profile gauge. With a pencil, scribe around the obstacle on the outside of the block onto a paper template. This template will already need to have been roughly cut to fit around the obstacle. Next, place the template over the vinyl (allowing for the depth of the vinyl to the skirting). Line the outer edge of the block up with the pencil

▲ Wide expanses of floor area can take bold patterns or design effects. Here, large vinyl tiles have been used in the same pattern combination in both the kitchen and the neighbouring room, emphasizing the space available. The kitchen walls have been matched to the red tile colour to provide a bold but harmonious link.

Cutting around obstacles

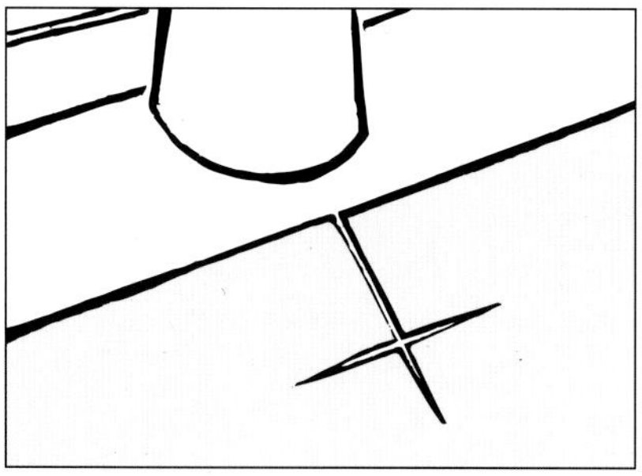

1 *Make two release cuts in the paper, at 90 degrees to each other, so that the paper can butt up to the wall.*

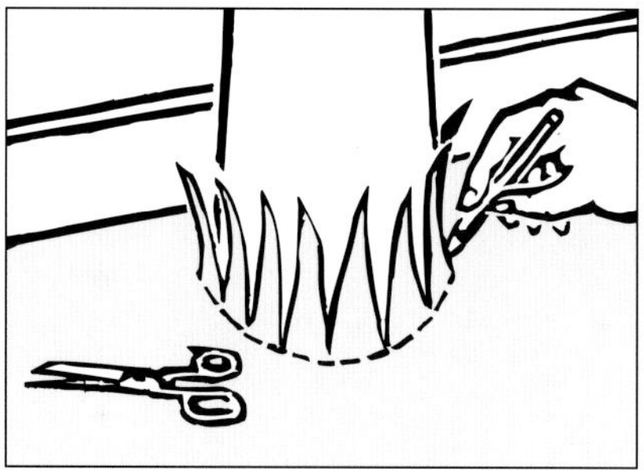

2 *Make more release cuts until the paper lies flat around the obstacle. Fold the flaps down, draw a profile and cut.*

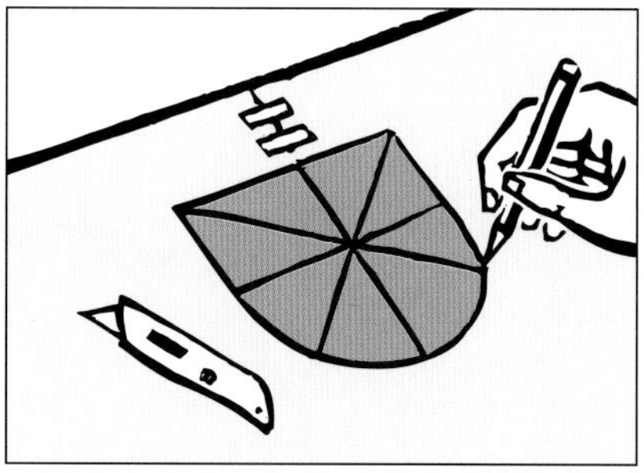

3 *Make two release cuts in the vinyl. Transfer the outline of the obstacle using the paper template and cut a hole.*

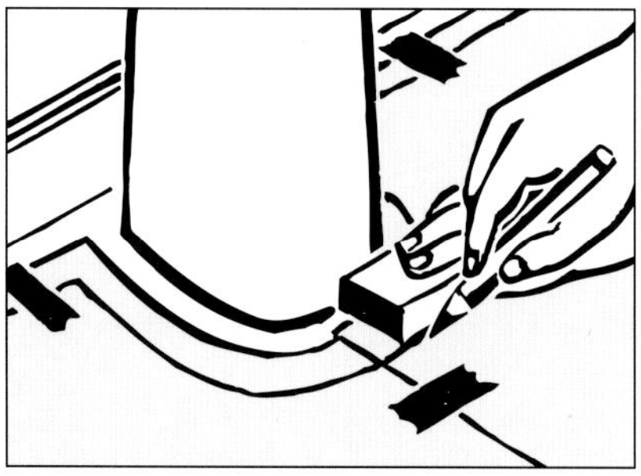

4 *Alternatively, use a wooden block to accurately scribe the profile of the obstacle onto your paper template.*

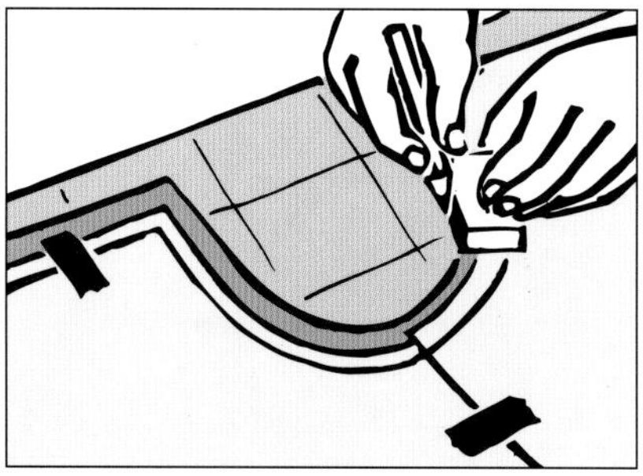

5 *Fix the template in position and, with a pen inside the block running around the profile, re-draw the outline.*

6 *To cut around a pipe, make a release cut, mark the pipe's position, and, using a coin as a guide, cut a hole.*

line you have drawn on the template and transfer the shape onto the vinyl, by scribing along the inside of the block as you move it around the pencil line.

To fit vinyl around pipes, make a release cut so that the vinyl lies flat at the wall. Measure the position of the pipe and fold the vinyl back from the wall. Measure the place on the vinyl where the hole is to go and mark it using an appropriately sized coin. Cut out the hole and refit the vinyl into place.

Cutting around doorways

Make a series of mini release cuts in the vinyl in the same way as for any corner so a flap fits between the sides of the doorway (see pages 52–53). Alternatively, use a profile gauge to copy the shape of the architrave, transfer this to the vinyl and cut it to fit. Or make a mini paper template. Otherwise, you can fold the vinyl back and carefully cut a sliver off the bottom of the architrave with the end of a long saw, taking care not to damage the surrounding floor. The vinyl can then be slipped underneath the architrave.

Finishing off

For a neater and longer-lasting floor, 'cold weld' any seams to prevent dirt and moisture from getting into the gaps. A solvent-based product, this glues the seams together. Always follow the manufacturer's instructions. Edges can be sealed using a silicone sealant; this is recommended in potentially wet areas such as around the base of a bath and sanitary ware in bathrooms. Fit a metal threshold strip over the edge of the vinyl at the doorway. If fitting mistakes have resulted in gaps at the edges, cover these with wooden beading.

◀ *In smaller rooms with limited floor areas such as kitchens, floors can be made to look bigger by using single-colour wall-to-wall coverings. Because vinyl can be cut to fit small room shapes from one large sheet, it is particularly suitable for kitchens, as food cannot be trapped between cracks and floor-cleaning is much easier.*

Laying linoleum and cork tiles

▶ *In a narrow hallway, work towards the edges of the floor from a centre line running down the entire length of the hall. Plan well and adjust the centre line as necessary before you start. Butt the tiles closely together and trim at the edges. Note the use of a threshold strip at the doorway to prevent the tiles being kicked up and damaged.*

Laying flexible floor tiles is an easy and straightforward job. The tiles are simply butted together without any need to grout or fill joints. They are easily cut to shape and are much easier to handle than their sheet equivalents. Tiles are also more versatile than sheets as they can be used decoratively: by incorporating a border, for example, or creating a focal point in the centre of a room.

With linoleum tiles it is possible to inlay a simple design. A straightforward chequerboard pattern using two colours, for instance, can be enlivened by insetting key squares at the centre of four big squares. Ready-cut designs can be purchased for laying or you can cut and lay your own key squares.

Before starting the work, prepare the floor as described on pages 34–35. It is particularly important for the floor to be absolutely level as even the smallest bumps or hollows will be visible on the finished floor and will spoil the effect. For the best result, use a latex smoothing compound.

If you are not using self-adhesive tiles, your supplier will advise you as to an appropriate adhesive. Unsealed cork tiles should be finished with a varnish as for floorboards (see pages 28–29).

Laying the tiles

Set out the floor as described on pages 38–39, although you should not really need to mark out a grid to cover the whole floor: being machine-cut, flexible tiles should – providing you follow the main guidelines – butt up against each other and remain square right up to the edges of the room. Begin in the centre and work towards the walls.

Use the correct adhesive for the materials. As a general rule, a water-based acrylic adhesive, which is free from unpleasant solvent fumes, is quite suitable. Spread the adhesive with a notched spreader of the size recommended by the manufacturer and covering only the area that you can comfortably tile before the adhesive spoils. Roll the adhesive smooth with a paint roller wetted with adhesive to minimize the risk of the adhesive pushing up under the tiles and showing through as ridges.

Self-adhesive tiles are much easier and less messy to lay. All you have to do is peel off the protective backing paper and place the tile in exactly the right position, before pressing it down firmly.

Place the first tile on the intersection of the two main guidelines and press it down from the centre outwards to expel any air that might be trapped beneath which could cause bubbling. Butt the next tile firmly against it and press it down. Clean off any adhesive from the surface with a clean rag. Tile one side of the room, laying the tiles in a pyramid pattern and working towards the wall. If the tiles that follow the main guidelines are correctly positioned, all the subsequent tiles

▲ *No cork tile is difficult to lay, but those that come with a self-adhesive backing are particularly convenient. Remember that unsealed tiles should always be varnished, and that prefinished tiles benefit from a coat of varnish if they are being laid in kitchens or dining areas where they need to be regularly mopped.*

should fall into place precisely; with factory-cut tiles there are always two edges to work from, ensuring that the tiles are laid square.

Fitting border tiles

When all the main tiles have been laid, start laying the border or edging tiles. Place a tile exactly over the last whole tile in a row. Lay another tile on top that so its edge butts up against the skirting board. Mark a line along the opposite edge on the loose tile underneath. Cut this latter tile along the marked line using a sharp knife and a straight edge; the trimmed-off piece should fit neatly into the border. Repeat the procedure for each of the rest of the border tiles. Any obstacles can be dealt with in the same way that they would be if you were laying sheet vinyl (see pages 54–55).

Laying key squares

Key squares not only add interest to a bland floor, they make a simple chequerboard pattern more sophisticated, and introduce a new colour into a flooring scheme with relative ease. If pre-designed, ready-cut materials are not available locally, you can cut your own key squares.

You can use the same technique to cut out other shapes such as stars, but remember that cutting out complicated shapes is a highly skilled operation and that it is all too easy to end up with gaps between the inlaid pieces. Before cutting up a floor, practise on some scrap pieces first or stick to simpler shapes.

Mark out the square onto stencil card and cut out the shape. Divide the square into four equal triangles with a pencilled cross. Place the stencil over the intersection of four tiles making sure it is correctly positioned with the lines of your pencilled cross aligning exactly with the lines between the tiles. Using a fine pencil, trace the outline of the key square onto the tiles. Then cut out the outlined square using a sharp knife; cut along the lines as carefully as possible and gouge out all the linoleum within the square. Use the same stencil to mark out a square on the linoleum you intend to inlay. Carefully cut out this square and glue it firmly into place in the appropriate position on the floor.

Laying soft flooring tiles

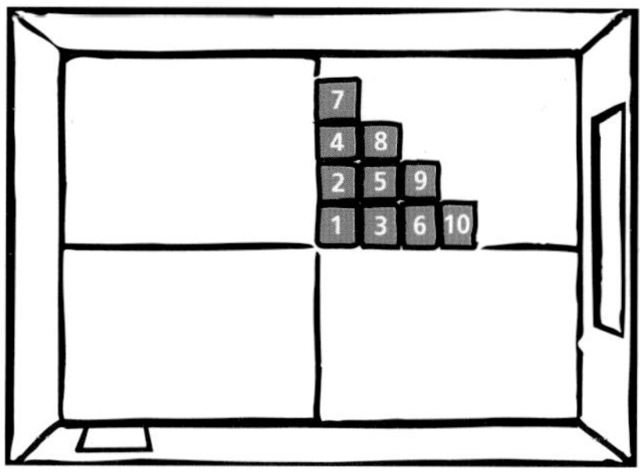

1 Having established and adjusted your centre lines, start to lay your tiles from the middle and work outwards.

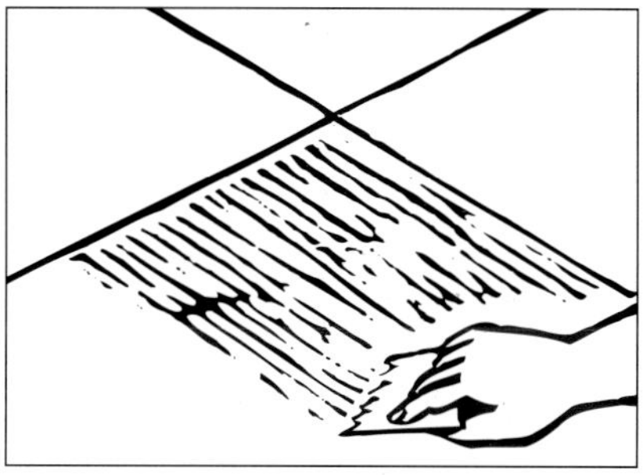

2 Spread the adhesive with a notched spreader; the glue must not be so ridged as to affect the surface of the tiles.

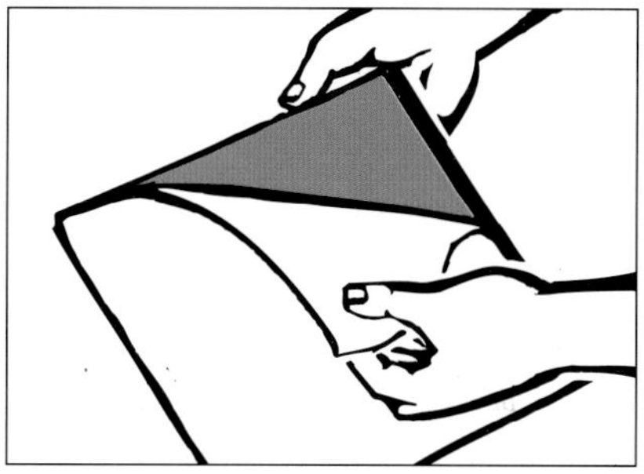

3 Alternatively use adhesive-backed tiles; they are less messy to lay. Peel off the backing and press into position.

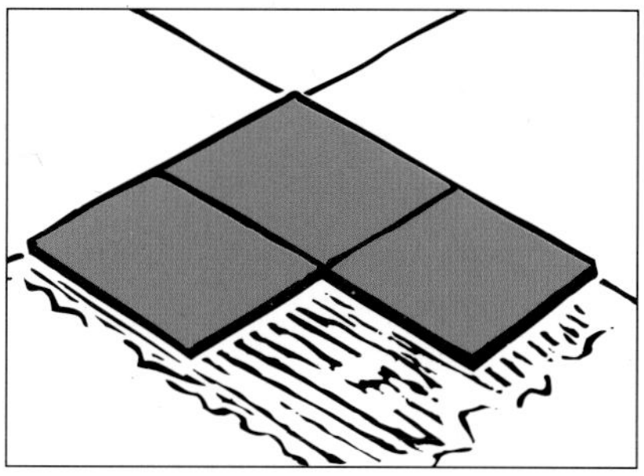

4 Position the first tile at the two guidelines' intersection and work outwards, smoothing out any trapped air.

5 To cut a border tile, lay one tile on the last whole tile, another against the wall, and mark the loose tile.

6 Cut along the marked line; the piece you trim off should fit neatly into the space at the border.

7 To position a key square, place the stencil on the intersection of four tiles and trace the outline in pencil.

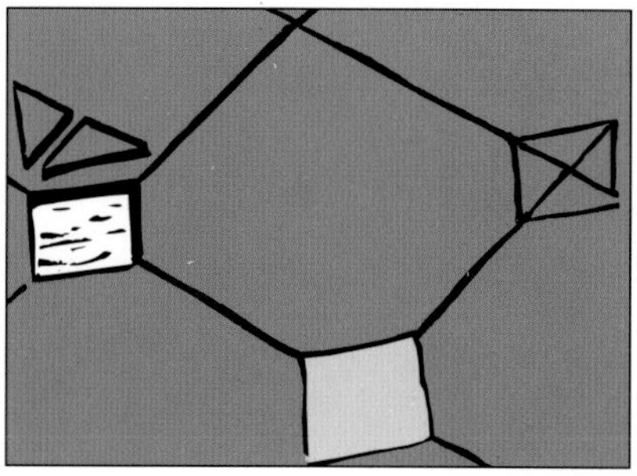

8 Cut out the outlined corners to accommodate the key square, spread glue on its back and press into position.

Decorative wood flooring

Wood has long been used for flooring, as it is so readily available as well as being an easily worked and practical material. Diverse, beautiful and with a natural complexity and depth unmatched by most other flooring, it is a material with infinite appeal. Its practical, easily cleaned and durable surface always feels warm and welcoming. The distinct elegance and luxury of new decorative wood flooring probably makes it the only flooring material that will look right in virtually any room in the home.

It is perhaps unwise, for practical considerations, to install wood floors in very wet environments; a bathroom that is continually soaked would not be an ideal place for a wood floor.

New sanded and sealed wood, without any distracting gaps between the boards, is particularly at home in a modern and minimalist interior, which relies on simple, clean shapes and the use of natural materials for maximum impact. But wood also suits any style of contemporary room. A more traditional, country room, on the other hand, might look better with old, wide boards that have moved and twisted over the years, leaving gaps and some imperfections. Yet, such is the never-fading appeal of wood that this type of floor could equally suit a more up-to-date scheme. And wood always ages gracefully, in most cases darkening and gaining character as the decades pass.

Each type of wood has its own distinctive colour and grain, ranging from pale ash to the near black of ebony, although this is too rare today to be used for flooring. In between are a multitude of warm browns, reds and rich beiges. Furthermore, wood can be stained for additional colour variations. The grain can be almost plain, with a few small flecks, or have wild, swirling patterns with great diversity in the colouring. The degree of patterning is dependent upon the type of wood but varies considerably within species. The plainer knot-free examples tend to be more expensive than types with a busy grain and some imperfections.

The colour range of wood is such that it will live happily with most other types of furnishing. The hues are generally muted and neutral. Plain wood is usually sufficiently interesting to be left as it is, although it provides the perfect backdrop for loose-laid rugs when a little extra splash of colour and warmth is desired.

Fortunately, wood is one of the easier flooring materials to install. Traditionally, wood planks are laid over timber joists but these days floating floors are widely used. All that is required to create a brand new floor in a matter of hours is for pre-finished boards to be fitted together over an existing subfloor.

Manufactured wood floors are nearly always made from a hardwood, even if the real wood element is only a thin veneer. The lighter-coloured hardwoods are traditional wood types such as ash, maple and beech. Beech and maple have a particularly unobtrusive grain, ideal for rooms where a light and plain-looking floor is wanted, which would not add any textural detailing to a room. Oak is a darker hardwood with a particularly interesting grain and it is widely used for flooring. Other darker woods such as walnut are sometimes used for floors, too, as are more exotic species such as mahogany and teak, which are a rich golden-red colour. Take care when choosing wood types; tropical hardwoods are likely to have come from non-sustainable primary forest.

All woods can be stained to change their colour. The lighter woods such as beech are frequently stained or have a semi-opaque lacquer applied, to lighten their colour even further. If you want a rich and warm tropical wood, a stained European variety can actually make a very satisfactory alternative. Quality can vary; the more expensive grades are sold knot-free and uniform in colour while the cheaper qualities can vary considerably in colour from board to board. All the hardwoods are sufficiently tough for domestic use, although some, such as maple, are much harder than others. The laminated products can be even harder than solid boards because the middle layer is designed to cushion shock. New pine, however, is very soft and can be dented easily.

◀ *Modern wood-strip floors have a clean simplicity that suits contemporary taste particularly well; the pale and neutral tones of the floor here show off the furniture without any unnecessary distraction. Available in a wide variety of colours and textures, wooden floors are stylish and practical and will complement almost any room.*

▲ *This room is perhaps typical of modern informal living. The floor is light-coloured with a discreet grain that provides an easily cleaned, non-allergenic surface which is warm and inviting at the same time. There is a rug to lend extra colour and comfort, while the rest of the furniture sits easily in the scene.*

Directory of decorative wood flooring

Manufactured decorative wood floors of all types can be supplied either unfinished or pre-finished. Unfinished floors are plain, bare wood, so that the floor is installed before it is sanded and lacquered. Although the wood is initially cheaper to purchase, the finishing costs must be added on when you are deciding what you can afford. Because installation is much quicker and less disruptive, pre-finished floors are very popular. A major advantage of pre-finished floors is that the finish is applied in factory-controlled conditions and is even. An acrylic lacquer is frequently used and this can be several millimetres (fractions of an inch) thick or have a subtly textured surface for greater slip resistance. Some pre-finished floors have wear guarantees lasting as long as 25 years, although guarantees of 5 to 10 years are more usual.

Solid wood

A solid wood floor consists of planks of wood laid across joists or over an existing subfloor. Traditionally, the boards would have been quite wide and straight-edged but most modern solid wood flooring is tongued and grooved. Tongued-and-grooved boards eliminate draughts from under the floor and make any shrinkage and movement of the planks less noticeable. The main advantage of a solid floor is that it can be resanded several times, making it an excellent long-term proposition.

Load-bearing wood flooring should be at least 18–20mm (¾in) thick, although wood being fitted over an existing subfloor can be as thin as 1cm (⅜in). Most manufactured hardwood floors are made up of quite narrow strips, 57–83mm (2¼–3¼in) wide, which means that any shrinkage is less noticeable because the gaps are smaller, and any warping of the boards is less pronounced. The boards can be either finished or unfinished. 1

1

Wood-block flooring

This type of flooring comes as tongued-and-grooved solid wood blocks 2cm (¾in) thick, which can be arranged in a variety of patterns. The most common arrangements are herringbone and double herringbone patterns with a straight border two blocks wide around the edge. There is also a brick arrangement, in which the blocks are laid side by side in a staggered fashion, or a basket weave, when alternate blocks are laid at 90 degrees to one another. The blocks have to be laid on an existing subfloor using a bitumen-based adhesive to make a very durable floor that can be resanded many times. 4

Laminated wood floors

This is man-made board constructed of several layers. The top layer is a veneer of decorative hardwood but the layers beneath are usually either plywood or blockboard, or sometimes cork. The great advantage of a laminated-board floor is that it is relatively cheap to produce because the hardwood layer can be as thin as 1mm (1⁄16in), although it is normally more substantial than this. Another advantage is its potentially greater directional stability because the laminated construction minimizes the movement of the boards once they have been fitted. Laminated-board floors are available in thicknesses ranging from 6mm (¼in) up to 20mm (¾in). The heavier grades can be sanded down several times.

This type of floor is generally pre-finished with a hard-wearing layer of lacquer. The finished effect is very similar to a solid floor although each 'board' is often actually two or three times wider than the laid floor would suggest in order to facilitate speedier installation. Some laminated floorings have become so sophisticated that it is debatable whether they are wood floors at all; there is one product available as 3mm (⅛in) strips that are glued down rather like vinyl tiles, the real 'wood' element of the floor being an extremely thin sliver of the product. 3

2

Parquet

Parquet floors are made up of individual wood blocks, which were traditionally 6mm (¼in) thick but

which are now usually 10mm (⅜in) thick. They are available in different sizes and types of wood.

Parquet can be used to create the same types of pattern as wood-block and even more complex designs such as 'parquet de Versailles'. The blocks can either be fitted to the subfloor individually or they are supplied as panels ready to be laid. There are some elaborate and sumptuous designs

3

4

5

which are, in fact, marquetry floors made up from small pieces of dark and light woods. The wood is laser-cut to size in a factory and comes ready to fit with a cotton backing that is glued onto the subfloor. Finely detailed borders are also possible: a Greek key pattern, for instance; and complex arrangements of stars and repeat patterns can be used over an entire floor. Needless to say, this type of floor is hugely expensive and definitely requires professional installation, but it is one of the most beautiful floorings available. 5

Wood mosaic panels

Wood mosaic is a very economical type of flooring. The small wooden blocks are either fixed to a backing material that holds the whole pattern together, or the blocks can have a paper fixing on their face that is removed after fitting.

The blocks are arranged in various simple patterns: basket-weave pattern, for example, or Haddon Hall. To fit wood mosaic, the panels are glued to a subfloor, normally in the same way as flexible tiles (see pages 56–57), although some are available with a self-adhesive backing. In addition, some types of mosaic panels are tongued and grooved so that the tiles slot together without the risk of high spots (one panel sitting proud of others) developing. Mosaic panels are supplied either pre-finished or sanded ready for subsequent varnishing. 2

Laying wood-strip flooring

The easiest type of wood flooring to lay is a floating floor where boards are fixed together but not attached to the subfloor underneath. The boards can be either solid or constructed of laminated-layers and are available in various thicknesses. The thicker boards last longer but do obviously raise the level of the floor more noticeably.

The subfloor needs to be reasonably level, although it does not have to be perfect. The new flooring can be laid over existing floor-coverings, even on a fitted carpet if it has a firm, close pile. Indeed, laying a floating floor over an old carpet in an upstairs room will increase the sound insulation between that floor and the room below. Equally, you can lay an underlay of some sound-insulating material such as cork – or a special foam. Concrete floors must be dry. If there is dampness coming up through the floor, it may be necessary to install a damp-proofing membrane (see pages 34–35).

Most wooden floors require a 10mm (⅜in) expansion gap around the edge, but check with your flooring supplier. Ideally, the gap is covered by the skirting board but if it proves too disruptive to remove the skirting board before laying the floor, the gap can be covered subsequently with wooden beading, or it can be filled with a cork strip. The boards should be laid parallel to the longest walls, so if the room is square, it is up to you which way you lay the boards.

Normally, the boards of the first row are laid full width and the boards of the last row are sawn down their length to fit. It is worth measuring the room before you start in order to calculate how wide this last strip will be, because if there is only room for a thin strip, the floor will look more balanced if you saw the first boards down the middle before you start, making both the first and last strips cut strips of a similar width.

▲ *The direction of the planking here draws the eye down the corridor into the room beyond. This not only looks better than a crosswise arrangement, but is easier to install. Floors such as this can be laid on almost any surface, providing it is smooth and level. For a neater finish lay the floor first and then fit items such as kitchen units and skirting boards.*

Laying the floor

Start laying the boards against the longest and straightest wall. Place 10mm (⅜in) wooden spacers against the wall for the expansion gap and lay the first board against them, with the grooved edge facing the wall. Apply a little wood glue to the tongue on the end of this first board. Slot the next board against the

Laying wood-strip flooring

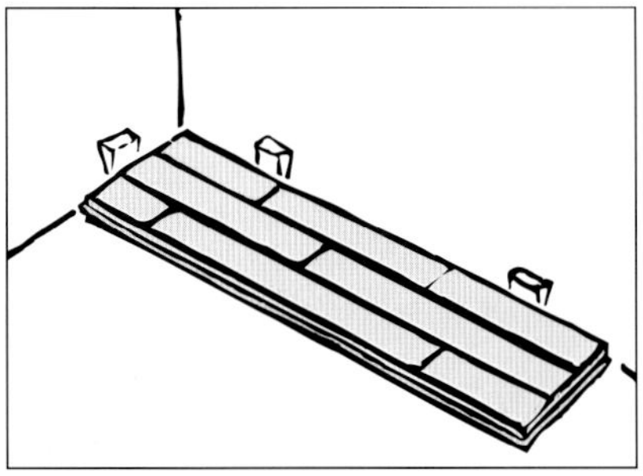

1 Lay the first board against wooden spacers, with a little glue on the end and the grooved edge facing the wall.

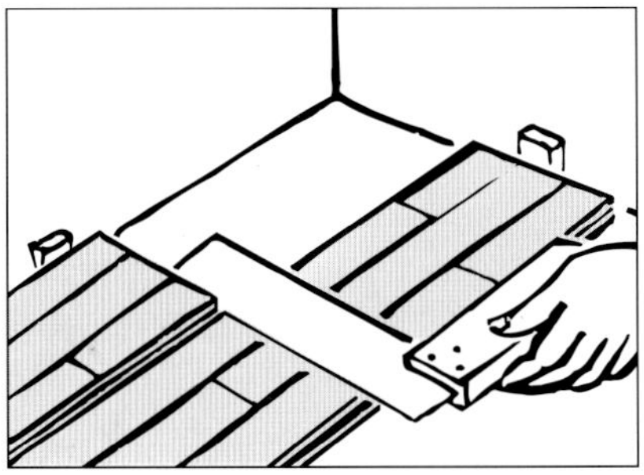

2 Turn the last board round, place it against the wall with a spacer, mark it in line with the laid board, and then cut.

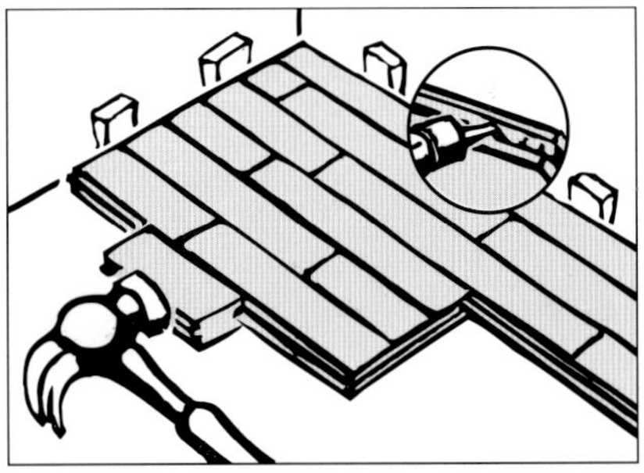

3 Use a hammer and an offcut gently to tap the glued second row of boards home securely.

Laying wood-mosaic panels

1 Adjust your centre point so that as many border tiles as possible can be trimmed in whole blocks.

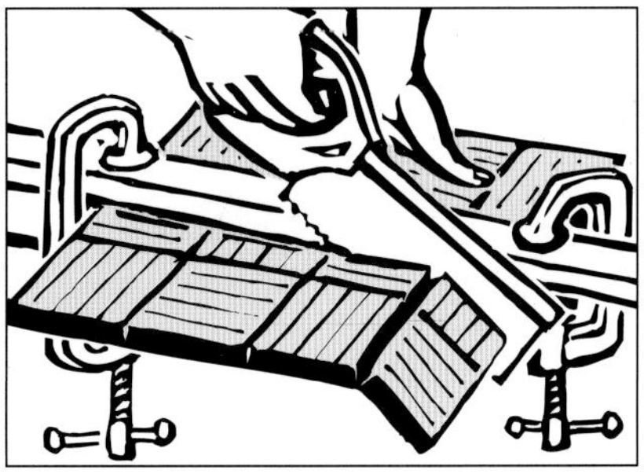

2 If you have to cut through the middle of a block, clamp the panel in place on a workbench and use a tenon saw.

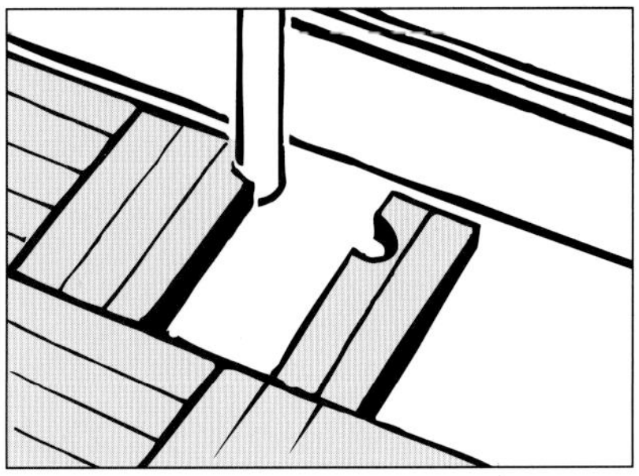

3 To fit neatly around a pipe, separate two blocks from the backing, cut two semi-circles and re-position snugly.

end of the first board and continue until you reach the last board along this row. To cut this board to fit, turn it round and place it against the wall, allowing for the expansion gap, with the tongue end facing the tongue end of the board already laid. Using a try square, mark the board to be cut in line with the edge of the laid board. Cut the board with a tenon saw, glue the tongue on the end and slot the cut board into position with the cut end facing the wall. Position wedges at both ends to prevent the boards from moving.

To prevent the joint lines creating lines across the room, which would spoil the floor's appearance, lay the boards with staggered joints – like bricks in a wall. Use the remainder of your first sawn board as the first board of your second row, with the cut end facing the wall. Apply a 10cm (4in) run of wood glue at 60cm (24in) intervals into the groove and push the board firmly into position. Using a hammer and softwood block or an offcut slotted into place, gently tap the board home. Wipe off any glue from the surface of the wood with a damp cloth. Continue working across the floor until you reach the penultimate row.

Position the first board of this row without any adhesive and then lay the last board on top so that it butts up against the wall allowing for the expansion gap. Run a pencil along the edge of the top board to mark the board beneath it. Remove the board and saw carefully down its length along the pencil line. Next glue the uncut board in place and finally the cut board – to complete the floor. Knock wedges into position to hold the floor tightly together until the glue has set.

To fit the boards around a radiator pipe, mark the board where the pipe will go and drill a hole (allowing room for expansion). Cut a V-shaped slot from the edge of the board to the hole. Lay the board and glue the cut-away piece back into place. The easiest way of fitting boards around an architrave is to place an offcut against the architrave and to cut away the base of the architrave. The board can be slid underneath the architrave for a neat finish. Alternatively, use a profile gauge (see pages 36–37) and cut the board so that it fits the profile of the architrave.

4 With the last board on top of an unglued penultimate board, mark the latter's edge on the board beneath; cut.

5 Mark the position of a pipe; drill a hole in the relevant position; cut a V from there; fix both cut piece and board.

Laying wood-mosaic panels

Wood-mosaic panels are easy to install. The technique employed is similar to that used for laying flexible tiles (see pages 56–57). You need to use an adhesive specially formulated for wood-mosaic panels, unless you decide to lay self-adhesive panels, in which you case you simply need to peel off the backing.

As the tiles are harder to cut than flexible tiles, try to adjust your centre lines so that at least some of the tiles around the edge can be trimmed in whole blocks – by merely cutting the backing between individual blocks. Where cutting through the wooden blocks is unavoidable, you will have to clamp the panel between a workbench and a wooden batten to immobilize the blocks and then use a tenon saw.

At a doorway, cut the bottom off the architraves as described for wood-strip flooring; or use a profile gauge and cut out the profile using a coping saw. The panels can be made to fit neatly around pipes by separating them from their backing at the point where the pipe is to go and then cutting two semicircles out of the blocks. Once fitted, these are held in place by the adhesive backing.

Soft floor-coverings

In cooler climates carpet is favoured for its warmth and is used widely for anywhere that requires bright colour and pattern, combined with a luxuriant quality. Once a luxury only for the better off, the invention of synthetic materials, coupled with steadily rising standards of living in the industrialized countries, has brought carpet within the reach of most people. Ironically, nowadays, carpet can be one of the cheapest and most practical flooring materials available.

Good-quality carpet is still costly and specially dyed, and woven wool carpet remains one of the most expensive of floor-coverings. Most wool carpets contain a proportion of nylon to increase their durability but cheaper carpets are generally made with a higher percentage of synthetic materials and are more loosely woven than traditionally made wool carpets. High-quality carpets, though, can be made from synthetic materials as well.

Carpet is, in fact, very hard-wearing and is suitable for most environments, including those that have to endure very heavy foot traffic; it is widely used in commercial applications. It is not suitable, however, where there are likely to be spillages – kitchens and bathrooms, say. If carpet is used in a demanding environment, it will need more expensive, specialized care than would a hard floor.

As carpet is such a forgiving material, the tendency in some countries has been to lay it in almost every room, but in recent years the sophistication of modern heating systems has meant that the sense of warmth afforded by carpet is no longer so important, allowing other materials, particularly wood, to gain in popularity. The recent increase in allergies to dust mites, which carpet harbours by the million, has also caused more people to turn to alternative flooring materials. For some rooms, however, carpet will always be a sensible and popular choice of flooring. Indeed, nothing can beat a fully carpeted bedroom in winter, feet sinking into the soft pile, warm and softly reassuring, even noise deadened to a soft hush. Inner sanctums – living rooms, studies – unlikely to be tainted by mud benefit too from that special sense of luxury.

Carpet is available in a huge range of colours and types. Darker colours are more suitable for areas, such as hallways, where dirt is likely to be brought in from outside, and you can choose from a vast range of neutral colours for a simple backdrop to an overall decorating scheme. Or you can make the carpet more of a focus. Borders, repeat patterns and central motifs are all easily incorporated into a carpet design. Stair carpet is available nowadays with attractive borders which can add restrained interest to an otherwise plain flight of stairs.

◄◄ The cool austerity of bare brick is considerably softened by the warm, deep pile of a luxurious wool carpet. This carpet has been made on a traditional narrow loom and has alternating patterned and plain strips with the same background colour. The strips indicate that this is a classic Axminster or Wilton carpet.

◄ Natural floor-coverings have become very popular recently. This formal drawing room is enlivened by the gutsy texture of rush matting which looks perfectly at home with all the different elements in the room. Note how this floor-covering is not fitted but stops just short of the walls, the edge being finished with braid.

Carpet is not the only type of soft flooring. Natural floor-coverings are increasingly popular, because they can provide a room with an elegant and sophisticated backdrop and are excellent for showing off colourful rugs. They are derived from plant fibres woven together to form a mat.

The fibres of natural floor-coverings are often left undyed, so they take their colour from the plant from which they are made. They may be bleached to offer a lighter, more neutral look. Although some plant fibres will not take dye, others can be dyed very successfully; sometimes an interwoven coloured weft gives the material a subtle hint of colour whilst retaining its overall natural, undyed look.

Part of the appeal of natural floor-coverings is their very definite texture. Some are quite soft and can be woven into fine patterns; others seem rough and hairy. These are used to create textured and robust patterns.

Natural floor-coverings are economical to buy but they do not always wear well and they can be very difficult to clean. It is worth buying matting that has been factory-treated with a stain inhibitor, although latex backing also makes day-to-day care easier and the matting can be laid like rubber-backed carpet.

There is also a range of wool-based floor-coverings made in new ways to consider. These combine the practical advantages and underfoot softness of carpet with the character and look of natural floor-coverings.

Directory of soft floor-coverings

Soft floorings fall broadly into two types: carpet, which is made from wool or a number of man-made fibres; and matting, which is made from plant fibres. The names given to carpet refer to the way the carpet is made rather than the materials used in its manufacture. The two broad categories of carpet are woven carpet, in which the pile is woven through a backing material, and non-woven carpet, in which the pile is attached to the backing by various methods using adhesives. Natural floor-coverings are plaited and woven to form strongly textured and patterned surfaces. The look and feel of each type of natural floor-covering derives from the special characteristics of the original plant. Incorporating wool fibres in natural floor-coverings is a recent development.

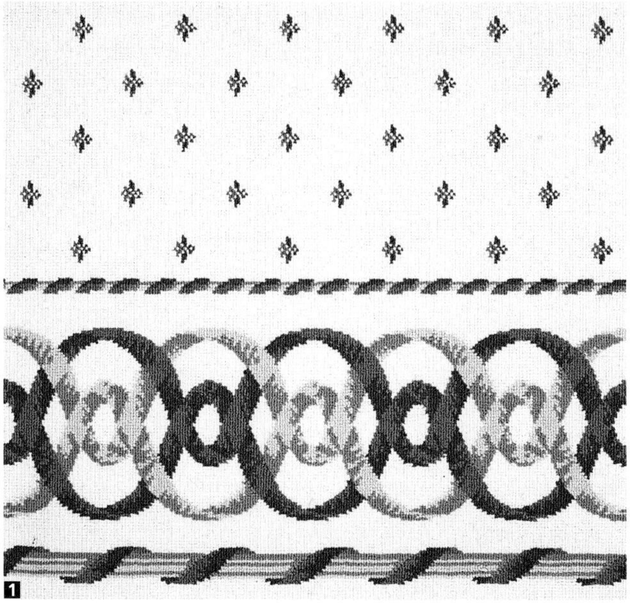

1

2

Woven carpet

Axminster

Axminster, one of the hardest-wearing types of carpet, is woven at the same time as the backing material, normally a natural fibre. The pile consists of a series of U-shaped loops threaded through the backing material. Latex or adhesive is often applied to the backing to help keep the tufts in position. A multitude of differently coloured yarns can be woven together into the carpet, giving unrivalled potential for complex colour and design combinations.

Wilton

Wilton carpet is woven at the same time as the backing material. The pile is made from a continuous yarn that weaves through the backing material and appears on the surface as a series of loops. The loops can be left uncut, which is known as 'Brussels weave', or cut to form a straight pile that resembles Axminster. Although the continuous yarn theoretically makes Wilton the strongest of carpets, it limits the design potential as only a maximum of five colours can be used together. Wilton can be woven as a textured design with two yarns, usually of slightly different shades of the same colour; one shade is a higher cut pile, the other is shorter and left looped to create a three-dimensional pattern. 1

Tufted carpet

In tufted carpet the pile material is woven into an existing backing material, usually a synthetic product, and held in place with a latex adhesive, before a second layer of backing material is fixed to the latex for greater structural strength. The backing can be either a natural product, which will require a felt underlay, or rubber, which can be fitted directly over the floor. Although not as strong as traditional types of carpet, the construction of tufted carpet is nonetheless effective and cheap to produce. Due to limited design possibilities, this type of carpet is usually plain or made up of two interwoven colours or a series of very simple dots or crude shapes. Designs can, however, be printed onto the surface for added interest.

Bonded carpet

Bonded carpet is made by fixing the pile to a ready-made backing with an adhesive. It looks similar to a plain woven carpet but uses less pile yarn as this is not woven in and out of the backing material.

Fibre-bonded carpet

In fibre-bonded carpet, fine, synthetic fibres are forced through a backing material with barbed needles, and are then fixed onto a fairly rigid backing, PVC, for example. This construction method produces a thin, coarse carpet without a conventional pile but with a hairy appearance instead. It is often used in commercial interiors.

Flocked carpet

Flocked carpet is made electrostatically: an opposing electrical charge between the pile material and the backing causes the pile fibre to be attracted to the adhesive-coated backing in an upright position, like hair standing on end. Patterns can be printed onto the short pile, which is easily cleaned, making flocked carpet ideal for areas subject to heavy soiling.

Carpet tiles

Carpet tiles consist of carpet attached with adhesive to semi-rigid backing squares. Their main advantage is that a damaged or worn area can be replaced without having to renew a whole carpet. Tiles from underneath furniture, for example, can be swapped with those in high-traffic areas to even out wear. They also allow easy access to under-floor wiring or plumbing. Extra replacement tiles should be purchased with the main batch, as those bought at a later date will almost certainly be a slightly different colour. 2

Natural floor-coverings

Coir

Coir is a fibre derived from coconut husks that is spun and woven to make a latex-backed floor-covering. Its coarse and hairy quality makes a strongly textured flooring material which can be woven into many different patterns – basketweave, bouclé, herringbone, diamonds – some wonderfully three-dimensional. Natural coir is a warm brown colour but a more neutral, bleached form is also

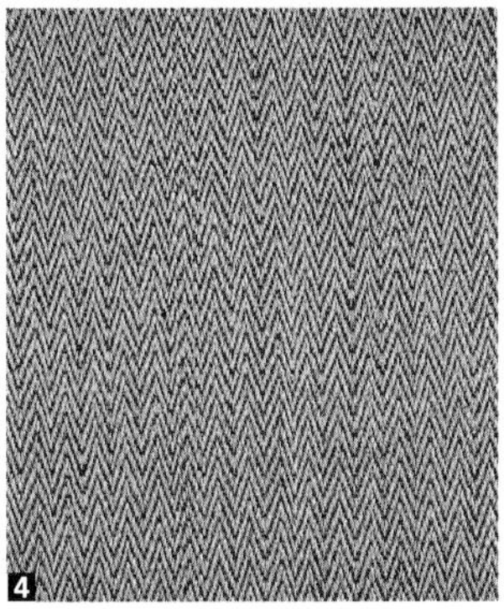

available. Coir can be dyed with plain colours, or several colours can be interwoven to create subtle two-colour weaves or vividly coloured stripes. Probably most familiar as the traditional doormat, it is indeed particularly suitable for areas of heavy wear such as hallways, as it is easy to clean with a stiff brush and vacuum cleaner. **3**

Jute

Although traditionally used as a carpet backing, jute is one of the finest and softest of natural floor-covering materials. It is made from yarn derived from the fibrous stalks of the jute plant and woven into either a bouclé or herringbone pattern. Naturally a pale neutral brown, it can be bleached to create a very pale cream, or dyed and then woven, rather like a carpet, to create simple coloured patterns. Different weights of yarn create finer or heavier textures. As jute is so soft it is ideal for bedroom floors,

but it is not a practical material for areas of heavy wear as it is difficult to clean and develops watermarks if it gets wet. **4**

Rush

Rush has been used as a flooring material since the Middle Ages when it was strewn onto cold flagstones to soften them. The wide, thin rush leaves are plaited and then woven into strips that can be stitched together to cover any width of floor. The edges can be finished with a finely woven rush braid. Rush matting is a pale, warm brown that can look fantastic in the right setting. It is more expensive than other types of matting and should only be used with care in areas of light wear. It should not be allowed to dry out otherwise it will become brittle and crack, so it is perfect for floors that are slightly damp; alternatively sprinkle it with water every week or two.

Seagrass

A grass grown rather like rice in wet paddy fields – hence the name – this is a hard yet smooth fibre that is woven onto a latex-backed floor-covering as a simple or a basketweave pattern. An excellent neutral colour in its own right – brown and beige strands with a definite green tinge – it cannot be dyed; the fibre is impermeable. Wefts of other colours can be worked in, however, to provide a hint of colour. Seagrass is a versatile and practical material that can be used in most situations. Because it is relatively non-absorbent and hard, it does not often stain and dirt is easily brushed loose. Freshly laid seagrass has a wonderful smell rather like new mown hay.

Sisal

From the leaves of a spiky bush rather like a yucca plant, sisal can be spun into yarns of different weights. It is woven into a variety of simple patterns that can look subtle or strongly textured depending on the weight of yarn. Unlike other floor-coverings, strands of sisal can be dyed before being spun, so it can be dyed as a plain colour or interwoven in two or more colours. Different colours are also spun into a single yarn to give the finished product a subtly coloured, metallic quality. It is also possible to paint sisal quite successfully; borders and all-over patterns can be applied either before or after the material is fitted. It is a durable yet gentle material that can be used for most situations. **5**

Wool-based natural floor-coverings

Made from wool-and-nylon mixes or a sisal-and-wool mix, these are a half-way house between carpet and natural floor-coverings. The fibres are spun into a heavy yarn and then woven into various simple patterns, as plant-based floor-coverings would be. There is no loose pile to speak of as the material is tightly woven, the aim being to create the robust texture of plant-based floor-coverings. At the same time wool-based floor-coverings have the advantage of being softer and more easily cleaned than their plant-based cousins. Neutral browns and beiges or subtle, washed-out brighter hues are the most favoured colours. Some have had a herringbone, bouclé or other weave dyed into the pile, which, from a distance, makes them look like textured materials but with an ordinary pile.

Laying carpet

Carpet is made from either natural wool or a variety of synthetic materials – rayon, polypropylene, or nylon – all with different properties that are used according to the carpet's function; the fibres can be mixed to combine their various advantages. Synthetic materials are cheaper than wool, and synthetic carpets can be very hard-wearing although their appearance may be less attractive. They also melt if a cigarette end is dropped on them. Wool is a natural, environmentally friendly product; it wears well and has an excellent appearance and superior insulation properties. Most wool carpets contain some man-made fibres for increased durability – usually 80 per cent wool: 20 per cent nylon. Quality is classified according to the carpet's suitability for a particular purpose: so, 'extra heavy' is very good-quality carpet appropriate for a tough, commercial environment.

All types of carpet are available in a range of widths up to 4m (13ft) to suit different room sizes. Wider, or broadloom, carpet is better for situations where seams are to be avoided, although some people prefer the look of narrow-strip carpet, associated as it is with the more traditional and exclusive methods of carpet manufacture.

The pile of carpet is either looped or straight. Looped carpet is usually woven from one long length of yarn that loops in and out of the backing material, while straight pile is made either by cutting the tops off the loops or by inserting short lengths of material into the backing so that the two ends stick up. Pile varies in length. Short-pile carpets resist flattening more readily. They tend to look good for longer, although this does depend on the pile density and material. Long-pile carpets feel more luxurious, although very long pile has gone out of fashion. One way of making the pile more resilient to flattening is to twist a wool yarn tightly while heating it, rather like crimping hair, before weaving: twist carpet appears more textured than a smooth, velvet pile and is a good choice for areas, like stairs, that have to endure heavy traffic.

Woven-backed carpet

Traditionally, carpet has a jute or hessian backing but sometimes it is woven polypropylene. Woven-backed carpets are laid over a rubber or felt underlay which helps to even out irregularities in the subfloor and also makes the carpet feel softer and more substantial. Rubber feels softer underfoot but felt is more resilient and thus a good choice for an uneven floor or a carpet that needs stitching together. A combination underlay combines the qualities of both.

Laying woven-backed carpet is a tricky task for the amateur; it is, however, a very quick operation for a skilled person and comparatively inexpensive. It is probably not, therefore, worth laying such a carpet your-

Laying carpet

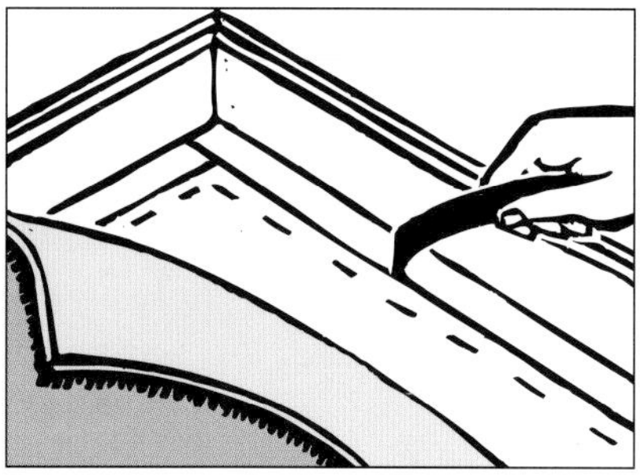

1 Fix underlay and tape to floor. Butt carpet against first wall, trim, and secure – removing backing from tape.

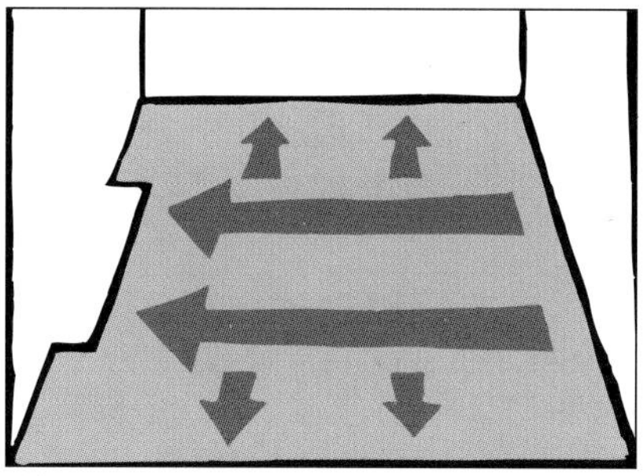

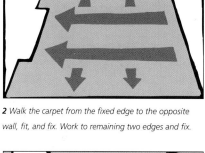

2 Walk the carpet from the fixed edge to the opposite wall, fit, and fix. Work to remaining two edges and fix.

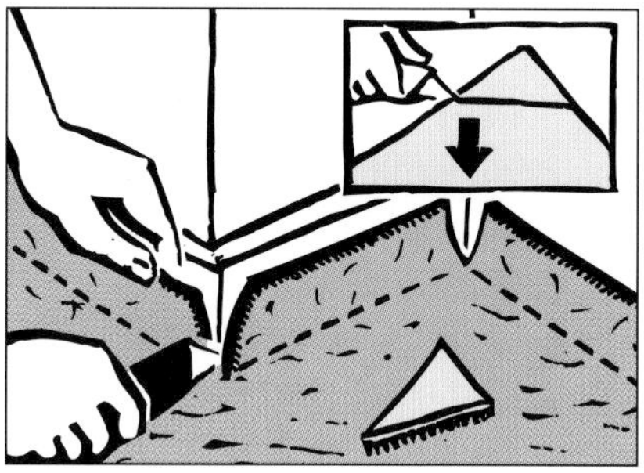

3 Make release cuts at external corners and trim diagonally at internal corners to ensure carpet lies flat.

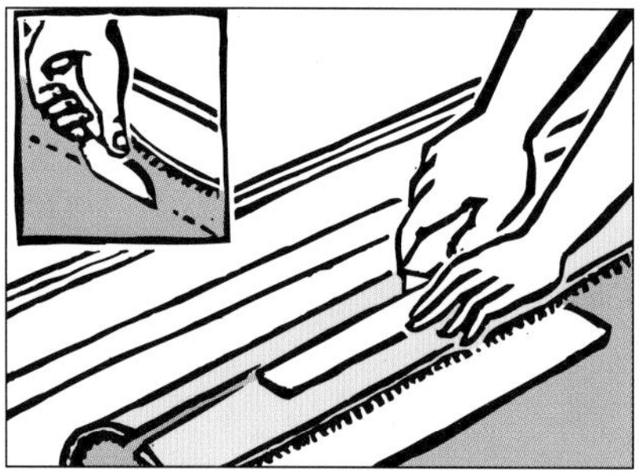

4 To trim, press into base of skirting with bolster chisel to score, turn back, and cut – on a board, along metal edge.

5 To make seam, bed one edge on length of carpet tape, butt up the next piece, and bond with seam roller.

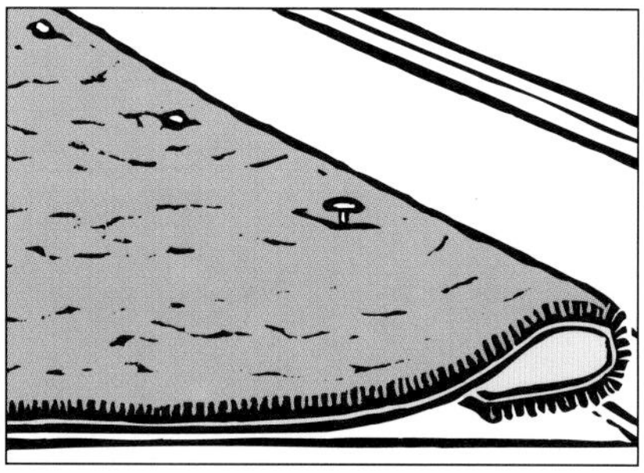

6 Alternatively, cut carpet slightly oversize, turn under and staple or tack through the double thickness to fix.

self, particularly as if it is not properly laid, unstretched woven-backed carpet will ruck up and wear very quickly.

Rubber-backed carpet

This is a cheaper type of carpet than woven-backed carpet; it has a rubber backing bonded to the carpet, which renders a separate underlay unnecessary. Felt paper is laid over the floor instead to stop the rubber sticking to the surface when the carpet is subsequently replaced. The main advantage of rubber-backed carpet is that it does not have to be stretched over gripper strips to fit. Having simply cut it to size, rather like laying sheet material (see pages 52–55), it can just be taped into position, although you can turn the edges under and tack it down.

Lay the paper underlay and apply double-sided tape down the longest, straightest wall. Keep the tape's backing paper in place, butt the carpet up to the wall, and trim it if necessary. Remove the backing paper from the tape and stick down this edge of the carpet. Stretch the carpet across the room to the opposite wall, fitting carefully at corners with release cuts, as necessary. Walk the carpet flat and trim this opposite edge to fit, before securing on a strip of double-sided tape as before. Finally, walk and stretch the carpet flat to the other sides of the room, and trim and fix these edges in position with tape.

Use a bolster chisel to press the carpet into the base of the skirting, and score a line along this junction. Turn back the carpet and cut along this line against a metal straight edge on a board. To make a seam, bed one edge onto a length of carpet tape and then butt up the first edge of the second strip. Press down the edges firmly with a seam roller.

If you prefer, tacks or staples can be used to fix the carpet edges. Having cut the carpet oversize, turn under excess and tack through the double thickness of carpet.

▲ *The rather stark look of this bedroom, created by the monochrome colour scheme and skeletal, twisted metal furniture, is softened by the addition of a thick, highly textured carpet with a woven diamond pattern. An expanse of snow-white carpet can create quite a dramatic effect, but bear in mind that such carpets rarely look spotless for long.*

Laying carpet tiles

***1** Mark the direction of the pile, place tile face down over the gap and mark the overlap by making slight nicks.*

***2** Cut tile, as marked, with a sharp knife on a board. Border tiles should be secured with double-sided tape.*

Carpet tiles

Carpet tiles are very easy to install. The principles for fitting them are the same as those for lino or cork tiles (see pages 56–57) except that carpet tiles should not be glued permanently in place. Use a tackifier adhesive that will fix the tile and yet will still allow it to be easily pulled up and repositioned. Alternatively, in areas where the tiles are likely to move and under heavy furniture, fix tiles using double-sided carpet tape. Make sure the pile all faces in the same direction, following the arrows marked on the back of the tile or running your hand through the pile to see which way it lies.

Border tiles are easily cut to size. Place the tile upside-down over the gap between the wall and the last laid tile, with the tile against the wall. Make two nicks on the tile, one on each edge, adjacent to the edge of the tile underneath. On a cutting board, using a craft knife and metal edge, cut the tile between the two nicks. Reposition the offcut at the wall; it should fit the gap exactly.

Laying natural floor-coverings

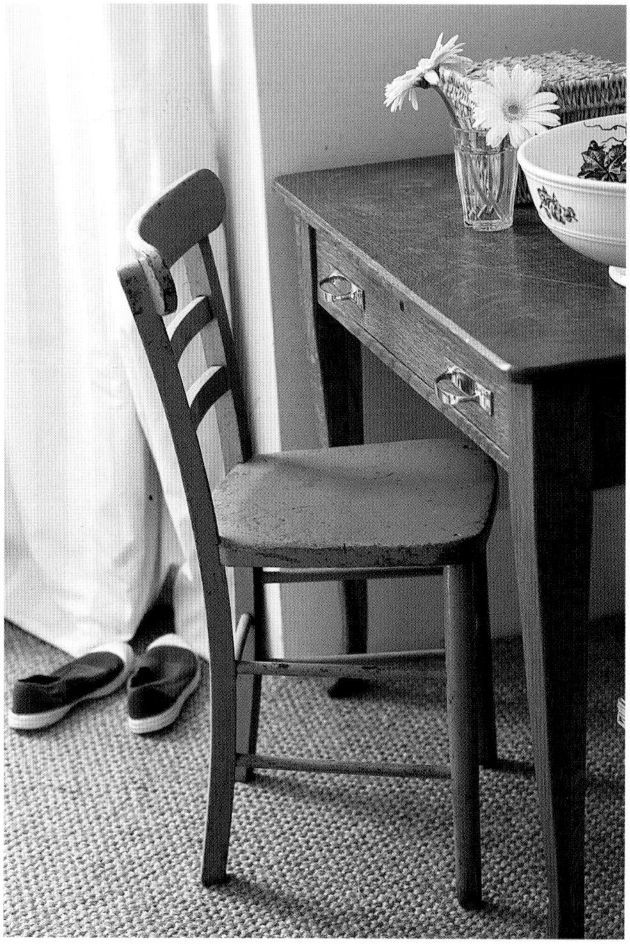

▶ *Sisal is versatile; it can be woven robustly, as here, or it can be finely woven. This basketweave sisal matting is installed in a similar way to a fitted carpet using gripper rods so that it fits neatly against the walls, and does not ruck up when the chair is moved. But natural floor-coverings are glued rather than stretched into position.*

When you buy a natural floor-covering – unlike many carpets – you will have to pay quite a bit extra for fitting and underlay. The labour cost can be much higher than for conventional carpet-laying because carpet fitters tend to dislike laying natural floor-coverings. As the underlays can also be quite expensive, laying your own natural floor-covering can make a significant saving.

Before embarking on such a project, however, bear in mind that some aspects are tricky. For example, some materials can be difficult to cut to size. They have to be glued to the underlay, which is stuck to the subfloor, and then gripper strips are installed to help hold the floor-covering in place and minimize any shrinkage. It is possible to lay natural floor-coverings without an underlay but the finished result will not be as comfortable to walk on and any slight irregularities in the subfloor will quickly manifest themselves as wear ridges.

Plan the laying before beginning work. Natural floor-coverings come in strips 4m (13ft) wide so that all but the largest rooms can be laid without a seam. Remember to add 7.5cm (3in) on to each edge for trimming. Any seams should run along the longest side of the room. Rooms more than 4m (13ft) wide will require another strip of floor-covering. If the extra width required is less than 2m (6ft 6in), you can order a strip half the length of the room. This can be cut down the middle and laid end to end for greater economy although it will mean that there will be an extra seam to live with.

Natural floor-coverings require no complicated sewing of seams. The seams are simply butted together, although the use of an extra adhesive bond is recommended on the joints. Always lay the floor-covering with the pattern of the weave running in the same direction. Unroll the floor-covering in the room in which it is to be laid at least 48 hours before fitting to allow it to acclimatize.

Laying the underlay

Begin by nailing or gluing the gripper strips into position 6mm (¼in) away from the skirting, with the gripper spikes facing the walls. Use a tackifier adhesive to secure the underlay to the subfloor. This type of adhesive does not go solid to form a permanent bond, but stays slightly tacky so the floor-covering can be lifted at a later date without damage to the subfloor. Apply the tackifier adhesive with a notched trowel or paint roller according to the manufacturer's instructions. Allow the adhesive to dry to clear, as specified by the manufacturer – depending on conditions, approx. 40 minutes. Unroll the underlay over the adhesive with the rubber side down and trim it to fit against the gripper strips; each length of underlay must butt up against the one already laid. Go over the floor with a carpet glider or a long-handled soft broom, pressing down firmly to ensure a good bond. The natural floor-covering can be laid over the underlay immediately.

Laying the floor-covering

Cut the material roughly to size, allowing an extra 7.5cm (3in) on all edges for trimming. If the room is more than 4m (13ft) wide, start at the wall furthest from the door and lay the material loosely into position on the floor. Mark the edge of the floor-covering with a pencil or chalk line as a rough guide for the application of the adhesive. Roll the floor-covering back on itself and away from the wall, without moving the whole piece, and exposing half the floor area. Use a suitable notched spreader and apply the correct amount of permanent carpet adhesive to the underlay. Some of the rough-backed floor-coverings, such as coir, will require the use of a coarse spreader which applies a greater quantity of adhesive in order to ensure a strong bond. Your supplier will advise you.

Carefully roll the floor-covering back over the wet adhesive and go over the glued area with a carpet glider to press the material into place. Now roll the unglued half of the floor-covering back on itself and repeat the process on the other side. If a second strip of material is required, only apply the adhesive within 20cm (8in) of the marked line. The second strip should be cut to length allowing the same extra 7.5cm (3in) for trimming, as described above. Then overlap the second piece over the first by 7.5cm (3in) and cut the excess from the wall, again allowing a margin for trimming. If a third strip is needed, the trimming will only be necessary on the final length.

The second strip can be glued into place as described for the first length starting from the seam. Remember to leave a 20cm (8in) strip at the seam without glue. Finally, glue the half-strip adjacent to the wall.

Trim the excess from the walls with a sharp knife, taking great care not to cut yourself with the knife or snag your hands on the gripper strip spikes which are very sharp. Fold the material against the skirting board and cut it along the base – against a board to protect the skirting – ensuring that you allow enough material to tuck into the gap between the gripper strip and the wall.

Trim the seam or seams using a straight edge and knife. Cut through both of the overlapping strips at the same time for a perfect finish. Place a piece of hardboard or plywood underneath the floor-covering to prevent the knife slicing into the underlay. Cut edges do not need binding because the floor-covering is backed, which prevents fraying. Fold back the edges of the seams and apply adhesive to the underlay and press the edges firmly down. Go over the whole floor again with the carpet glider or broom, or a roller, to ensure the floor-covering is firmly bedded into the adhesive. Finally, use a bolster chisel to press the material home at the edges for a neat finish. In a doorway a binder bar is a safe and easy option. Fix the bar in position adjacent to the doorstop, mark the position of the centre line on the floor-covering and trim. Press it in place under the bar with a bolster chisel.

Laying matting

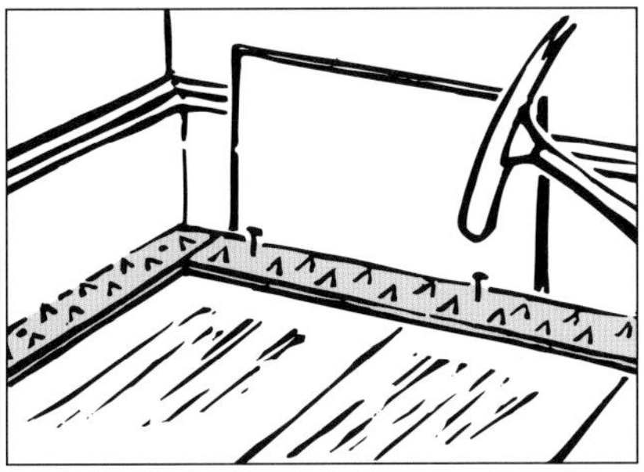

1 Secure gripper strips close to skirting, spikes facing the wall; if nailing in place, use cardboard to protect skirting.

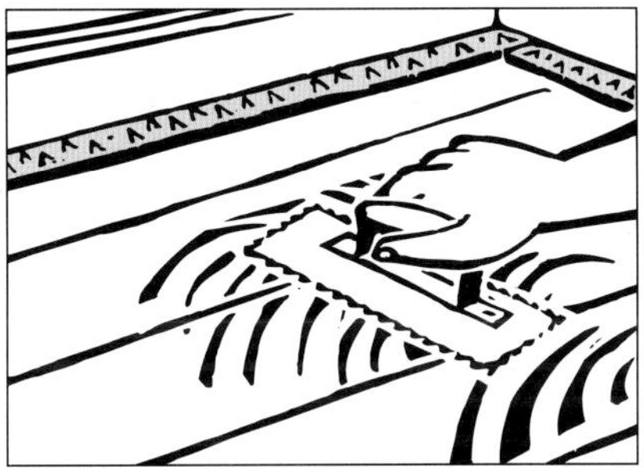

2 Apply tackifier adhesive with notched trowel up to the strips to fix the underlay to the subfloor; let dry to clear.

3 Lay the underlay rubber-side down and trim to fit against gripper strips; press firmly for good bond.

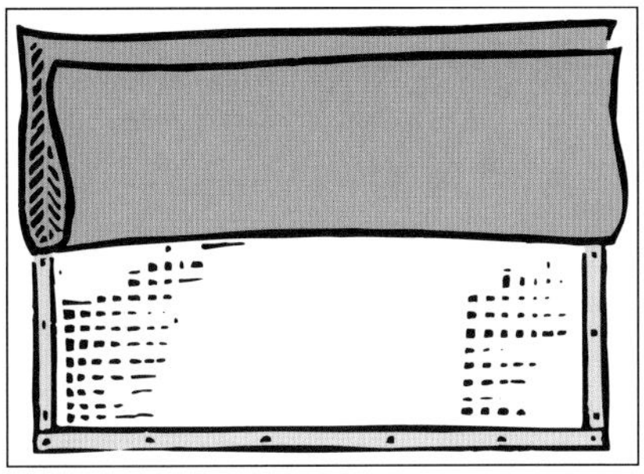

4 Roll back material on itself, apply adhesive on exposed half, roll back matting, and press. Repeat with other half.

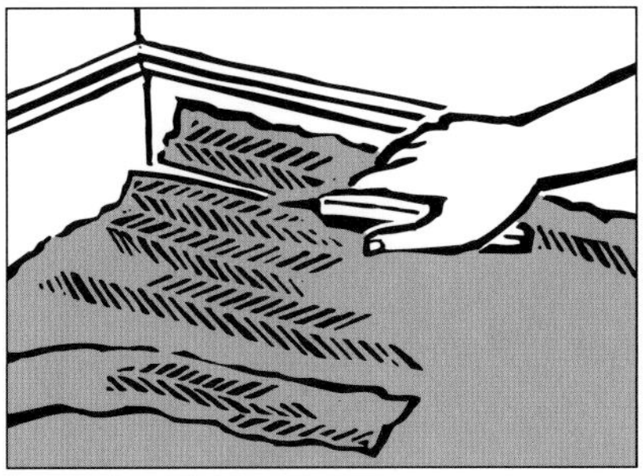

5 Taking care to avoid gripper spikes, trim excess with sharp knife at base of skirting against a protective board.

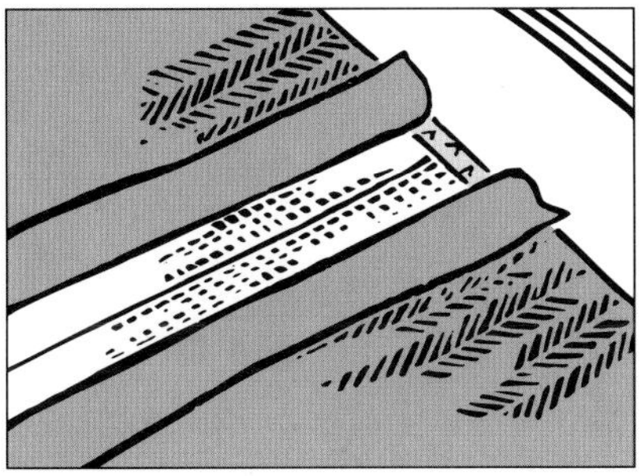

6 For a seam, overlap two strips, and cut through both layers onto a board. Fold back, glue and press into place.

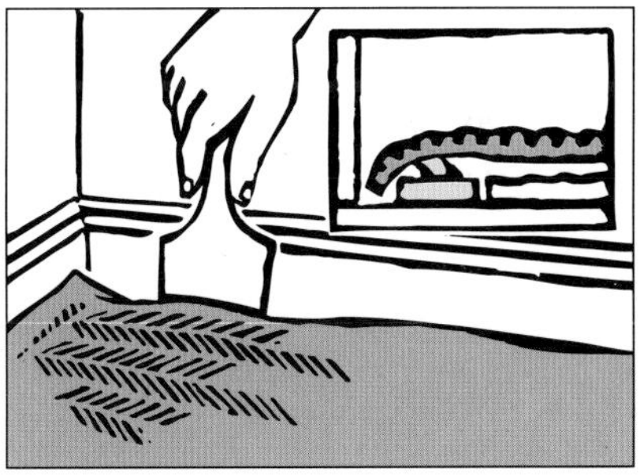

7 Use a bolster chisel to tuck the trimmed floor-covering snugly into the gripper strips at the edges for a neat finish.

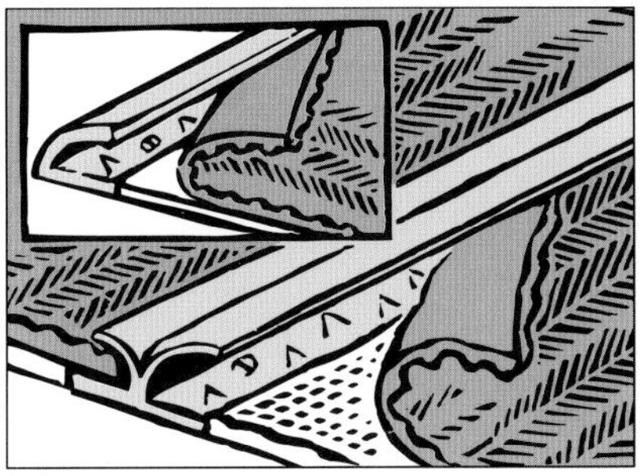

8 Cut binder bar to length with a hacksaw, nail in place, trim floor-covering to fit and press home with a chisel.

Unfixed flooring

The weaving of carpets and rugs is an ancient tradition embraced by virtually every society in the world at some time, whether small independent groups of nomadic tribes or a large collective society. Rugs and carpets are made for a far greater diversity of reasons than any other type of floor-covering. Rugs afford warmth and a degree of comfort for people inhabiting colder climates and mountainous regions and also make an important aesthetic contribution to any environment regardless of its physical location.

Most carpets and rugs are constructed from one of two types of weave. Tapestry or flatweave rugs have no pile. The weft is woven over and under the warp threads and pulled tight. Pile or tufted rugs, on the other hand, have a softer and more luxurious surface and are made by knotting individual strands of wool into the warp. In tufted carpets, the number of knots per square inch determines the fineness of the weave. Carpets with a high number of knots per square inch can incorporate intricate curved or floral designs and will also feel softer to the touch, while those with a lower density of knots per square inch are generally characterized by geometric designs.

Traditionally, carpets were dyed with natural dyes derived mainly from local plants, but today both chemical and vegetable dyes, or a combination of both, are employed. Natural dyes are considered superior because they give softer and more attractive colours that age gracefully, although it is possible to find exceptional chemically dyed rugs that have the same qualities.

Most countries have their own distinctive design traditions. Carpets from the East usually follow a design style and colourings peculiar to the tribe or region of origin of the carpet. Designs in the West tend, instead, to reflect the style of a particular period. Architects and designers have often tried to design rugs and carpets alongside their more usual occupations: Morris, Voysey and Mackintosh, amongst many others, all produced a wealth of rug designs. Today rugs can be very modern and free-form in style; many are arguably artworks for walking on.

Because a large carpet is inevitably a major focal point, it is better to purchase a fine rug first and decorate a room around it than the other way around. Carpets look best when placed over a neutral background; both wood and natural floor-coverings such as seagrass make a perfect backdrop, and stone can also look very sophisticated. Rugs can be used to provide a simple focal point or relief in a large floor area or to provide a greater sense of warmth and softness on an otherwise hard and unrelenting flooring material.

Buying carpet and rugs

Buying a carpet is something that should be approached with great care. Beware of spending a huge sum on a carpet because the carpet trade is like the secondhand car market: some carpet dealers can only be described as of somewhat dubious character. It can be extremely hard to tell if you are buying a genuine antique or a modern copy; equally, it can be difficult to distinguish between natural and chemical dyes, and the former would nearly always add to a carpet's desirability – and price! It is better to go to a reputable dealer who will give you a fair deal. It is also probably more sensible to buy a carpet from a reputable source on home territory than when on holiday; it may well be possible to secure a bargain when travelling but equally you might end up with something that could be purchased more cheaply and easily at home.

Backings and fixing

Although it is possible to put a rug straight onto the floor, it will last longer and will not move around if it is placed on an underlay. This is particularly important on wooden floors, as rugs are potentially dangerous if not held in place. The underlay used with fitted carpet can be used but the corrugated types should be avoided for thinner carpets, especially the thinner flatweave rugs like kilims, because you will see and feel the corrugations through the carpet. Generally, dedicated rug underlays are better, as these are specially designed to prevent the carpet physically moving on the floor.

While giving added protection from high heels and general wear and tear, particularly if the carpet is lying on a hard surface, underlay will have the added benefit of giving the carpet a softer feel. Thinner varieties can be obtained for use over a fitted carpet.

◀ *Wall-to-wall carpets are not everyone's preference, but while bare floorboards are wonderful in summer, they can look cold and stark during the winter months. This is when rugs, the most adaptable of all floor coverings, come into their own. This thick, hard-wearing rug with a chequerboard weave would help to ward off winter chills.*

▲ *A quirky interior, with more than a touch of the surreal, called for an unusual floor covering. This white rug decorated with parallel lines of black spots has a trompe l'oeil twist: the two spots in the centre have been cut out and replaced with plastic veneer to give the illusion of wooden flooring beneath.*

Directory of rugs and carpets

Flatweave carpet and rugs

1

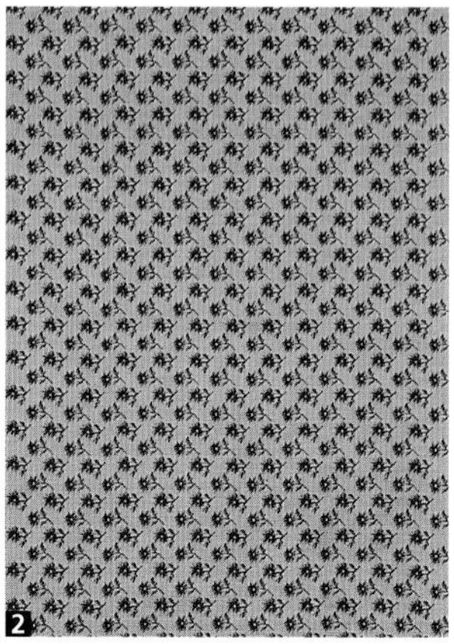

2

3

Kilims

Kilims are flatweave rugs made from wool. The term usually applies to rugs that come from an area stretching from Eastern Europe through Turkey and Iran to as far east as Afghanistan. For many years considered the poor relation to hand-knotted carpets, kilims became popular in the 1960s when the bold, bright colours and simple geometric designs appealed strongly to the hippie culture of the time.

Kilims can be woven much more quickly than a tufted carpet – important to nomadic peoples who were constantly moving on. Designs are much simpler and more geometric than those of the knotted carpet because of the limitations of the type of construction. Kilims frequently contain a series of slits, which occur when one colour of yarn adjoins another along a warp thread. Designs incorporating a series of long vertical lines are thus avoided as the length of resulting slits would weaken the kilim. Usually created using horizontal and diagonal lines with very short verticals, designs vary according to origin: Anatolian kilims are very colourful with particularly abstract geometric patterns, whereas traditional eastern Bulgarian kilims have a predominant black background characterized by floral motifs rendered in pinks, beiges and gentle yellows. 1

Dhurries

The dhurry is the traditional flatweave rug of India. Dhurries are made from cotton rather than wool, giving them a slightly harder quality than a kilim. As the dyes are taken up differently by the yarn they tend to be less brilliantly coloured than their wool cousins. Traditionally there were three types of dhurry: the bed dhurry was placed under a mattress; the prayer dhurry was divided into a series of prayer niches; and the room dhurry was intended for use in rooms. This latter type was the largest and could be enormous. The finest dhurries were woven in Indian prisons between 1880 and 1920 – an enlightened policy designed to relieve the monotony of prison life. Sometimes carpet designs were copied from imported Persian or Afghan carpets by prison warders or their wives, or new designs were drawn. Because of the influence of colonialism, traditional folk design tends to be watered down. Mosques or Hindu shrines appear frequently, although they tend to be quite geometric due to the construction of the dhurry. Today, dhurries are manufactured in factories for the Western market and are characterized by insipid pastel colours and sparse designs.

Needlepoint

Needlepoint is the sewing of a yarn, usually wool, using a variety of different types of stitch, into a ready-made canvas backing. During the eighteenth century in England needlework carpets enjoyed some popularity. Copies of traditional designs are made today in needlepoint as very few of the originals survive, along with designs associated with other types of carpet, in the style of the French Aubusson, for example. The origins of this particularly elegant and sophisticated style were tapestry-woven carpets made almost exclusively for French royalty and aristocracy, which as a consequence makes the originals rare and extremely valuable.

Needlepoint is also used in the recreation of other eighteenth- and nineteenth-century European designs and for creating original work as well, although many of the rugs are likely actually to be made in places such as China where labour costs are low. 2

Tufted carpet and rugs

Gabbeh

The gabbeh is a rug woven by the tribes of southern Iran. They are quite unlike more traditional Oriental carpets as they are woven for personal use in a much freer and more spontaneous style, their designs often taken from the weaver's immediate surroundings. Animals, birds and people and simple shapes such as diamonds or the tree of life also feature, the motifs often being used more sparingly than on traditional carpets with larger areas of plain colour. Largely made in factories now to satisfy Western demand, gabbehs are made from either natural or dyed wool, left unclipped and shaggy.

Floral carpets

A 'floral' carpet is a carpet that makes use of curvilinear design, as opposed to rather more geometric representations and patterns. This can only be achieved by the use of a very high density of knots per square inch,

4

which produces highly complex and fine designs. Carpets of this type, such as the 'Persian' carpet, are manufactured in more organized workshops from designs produced on paper by a designer. It is then woven into a carpet by a weaver who has little to do with the design process. Carpets made in this environment used to be produced almost exclusively for sale and export, often for the Western market. They are characterized by highly sophisticated and intricate designs of a very delicate nature, often produced using very dark and rich colours.

Geometric carpets

Geometric carpets are principally produced by tribal peoples, either nomadic or living in villages. The designer is also the weaver and the carpet design is made up as it is woven, although unlike the gabbeh mentioned above, the design uses traditional patterns and motifs. Each of these carpets is unique and is made for the use of the particular tribe. Some will be made for sale, and this is becoming increasingly common today as these smaller peoples enter the global economy. Tribal carpets originate from a huge area stretching from Turkey through Iran to Afghanistan. Each region or tribe has its own distinctive designs and colour range, although some motifs are universal and are also utilized in floral carpets.

The reason for this type of design is cultural and is in some part due to the difficult conditions under which the rugs are made. Tribal rugs are less formal and looser in style than floral carpets. More folk art than classical art, this type of rug is rather more suited to contemporary interiors than the manufactured carpets; consequently they are much in demand.

Contemporary carpet

These are modern carpets produced by artists and designers – art for the floor. They are produced for their own sake as purely decorative pieces, unlike some of the more traditional types of carpet. Designs vary widely according to the style of the individual designer, and can be entirely free-form and expressive, or more representational, either with or without borders. Some of these rugs are woven in the traditional carpet-producing areas of the East using hand-knotted wool and vegetable dyes, like the more traditional carpets of these regions. There are very few hand-woven carpets produced commercially in the West today as labour costs are so high. This type of carpet may well be made in China or India, or in other parts of the East, and indeed, most patterned rugs (whether designed or plain) originate from these areas. **4**

5

Fabric rugs

Rag rugs

The early American settlers living in more remote areas produced many of their own goods, rugs being one such item. These people were very frugal and consequently were very good at recycling materials. As a result they made rugs from strips of cloth obtained from clothes that had reached the end of their useful life and wove these into rugs of several different types. Rag rugs were the most common type of rug and were made from narrow strips of cloth that are woven on a loom, rather like a flatweave rug. The rug can be made from a fabric of one colour or other colours can be incorporated. Rugs of this type have a simple knobbly appearance that is a very cheap and effective way of covering up a bare floor. Today, rag rugs are easily found, but are likely to be made in places such as India. **3**

Braided rugs

Three or more strips of cloth are plaited together to form a braid rather like a person's hair. These braids are then joined together to make a rug. This type of rug would be started in the middle and worked outwards, with more braided lengths added to the outside of the rug until the desired size was reached. This type of rug was often circular or oval. The colour of the rug is dependent upon the colour of the cloth used in making the braid. The overall colour of the rug is controlled by varying the colours of the fabric used in each subsequent braid and in this way a pattern can be built up. Today this type of rug is often machine-made, although it is possible to make a rug at home in the same way that the original settlers did.

Hook rugs

Hook rugs are pile rugs made by pulling a yarn or a strip of fabric through a backing material using a hook. The pile is made from a series of fabric loops that can be varied in height to create either a firm, close pile or a longer, more shaggy look. The pile lengths can be varied on the same rug to create a more sculptured appearance. The hoops can be clipped in the same way as a Wilton carpet to create a soft, more velvety feel. Quite complex designs can be achieved using this technique, depending on the density of the hoops and the number of colours used. Representational rugs, more abstract patterning, or copies of oriental designs can be tried. Hooped rugs can look more sophisticated and less folksy than the other types of rug made from recycled materials, but this will obviously be dependent on the design used. **5**

Floorcloths

Floorcloths are an alternative to conventional carpets and rugs. They are really the forerunners of linoleum which, in turn, was displaced by vinyl. Floorcloths were popular in the eighteenth century as they could be painted to imitate expensive pile carpets. Sailcloth was the material generally used; it was given many coats of linseed oil to create a very heavy and durable surface. Floorcloths could be left plain or painted with a design. They were used in corridors and hallways, indeed any area of heavy wear that would have quickly ruined a carpet or rug and in the servants' quarters where a real carpet would have been considered extravagant. The great advantage of a floorcloth is that it can be painted with any imaginable design at minimal cost. Moreover, it is a surprisingly hard-wearing 'carpet', making it an excellent choice for a hallway runner. And it can be made to fit any particular room's shape.

▲ *A floorcloth makes a stylish and original alternative to a carpet or rug. The turquoise blue used here was probably specially mixed to offset the warm ochre used on the walls, while laying the cloth over grey colourwashed boards shows off both the colours and the design to maximum effect. In fact, the floorcloth forms the focal point of the room.*

Making a floorcloth

Preparation

A floorcloth is really a blank canvas onto which any design can be painted, rather like an artist paints a picture, except that the floorcloth requires a protective coat of varnish once the design has been completed. Artist's canvas can be used but it is probably better to visit a theatrical scenery supplier and buy the canvas from them, or to buy cotton duck, as this is a satisfactory, inexpensive alternative.

You can make a very large floorcloth as it is possible to buy cotton canvas up to approx. 9.5m (10½yd) wide and any length, although some of the cheaper alternatives may be a little narrower. You will need to buy a piece of canvas slightly larger than you expect the finished floorcloth to be because the canvas will shrink by approx. 7.5 per cent once it has been primed. You will also need to allow 2.5cm (1in) extra all round to fold under as a hem – to make a neat edge.

It will be necessary to find a space larger than the floorcloth in which to work comfortably. Begin by ironing out any creases in the canvas with a conventional steam iron. The canvas should be stretched before priming otherwise there is a risk of it rucking up unpredictably once it has been painted. A frame like an artist's stretcher can be made up to the required size using 5 x 2.5cm (2 x 1in) timber and the canvas fixed to that; otherwise pin the canvas along the edge to an existing smooth and level floor using plenty of drawing pins, though these will leave small holes. The canvas should be sized before painting; traditionally, artists use an animal skin glue that is purchased in granular form. A quicker and easier alternative is to brush the canvas with a modern PVA adhesive and then let it dry. Now prime the canvas with two coats of ordinary acrylic wood primer/undercoat, allowing two hours between coats; it is a good idea to give the underside of the canvas a coat too as this will give the floorcloth greater rigidity. The canvas will shrink so that it becomes very taut. Only at this stage can the drawing pins be removed, or the canvas be taken off its stretcher. Use a metre rule and pencil to mark out the size and shape of the finished floorcloth and additionally mark a second line about 2.5cm (1in) away from the first line towards the edge of the floorcloth. Cut away any excess material beyond this line. Use a sharp craft knife and a long metal rule and score along the first line – very gently, just to break the weave of the fabric – and cut diagonally across each corner on the marked line. Apply a fabric adhesive or PVA up to the marked edge and fold it on the scored line to give a neat, finished edge. The floorcloth is now ready for painting.

Painting the floorcloth

Almost any design can be painted onto a floorcloth; as usual, the only limiting factor is the skill and patience of the painter. Indeed, there is no reason why a full-scale painting cannot be created on the floorcloth; it is, after all, a blank canvas. It is probably better to stick to conventional rug designs used on a floor or to copy a picture of a real rug that you particularly like but cannot afford to buy. Simple chequerboard or grid-type patterns can be painted rather as they would be on a wooden floor: decide on the width of the border and mark it out using a pencil and ruler and then mark out the squares onto the centre of the floorcloth. If the floorcloth has one predominant background colour, paint the entire piece with that colour first before marking out the design. Floorcloths should be easier to paint than real floors as they are usually smaller and more manageable; the smallest floorcloths can even be painted on a table. More complex designs will need to be carefully planned and drawn out on the canvas, while complex borders or repeat motifs may be more easily painted using a stencil (see pages 22–23). As with painted floors, the paints themselves do not take any wear so you can use either artist's oils or acrylics, both for tinting colours and for painting in fine detail. You can use either oil- or water-based paints, either as opaque colour or, for a softer, more washed-out look, semi-transparent tones.

Finishing

Once the paint has dried, the floorcloth must be varnished. Use an acrylic varnish or an oil-based polyurethane, but remember that this latter will yellow with time. It is better to avoid floor lacquers as these are very hard-wearing but rather brittle and may crack. The floorcloth should have at least three coats of varnish – or more, if it is going to be subjected to especially heavy wear.

Once the varnish has dried, the floorcloth can be placed in its final location. If this is a hard surface (wood or tiles), it is best to stick the floorcloth down with a few squares of double-sided carpet tape to minimize skidding and to prevent the edges of the floorcloth from being continually rucked up, which will eventually cause the edges to curl and the paint to crack. Or try attaching an underlay as you might to a rug, because this will not only prevent slippage but also give the floorcloth a more luxurious, padded feel.

▲ *Floorcloths make particularly effective runners, though they can be made to fit any space. The plain yellow floorcloth warms the walls in this hallway, while the one in the foreground is embellished by a simple and effective design that picks up on the wall colour for a delicate balance, making it the epitome of discreet classical style.*

Making a floorcloth

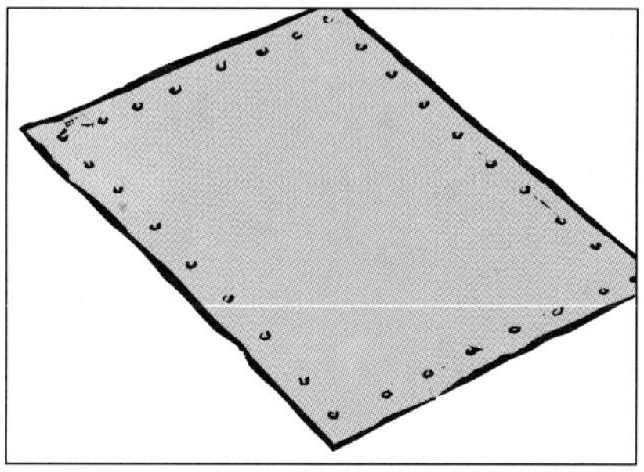

1 *Having ironed the canvas to get rid of any creases; fix it flat with pins along the edges – or on a stretcher.*

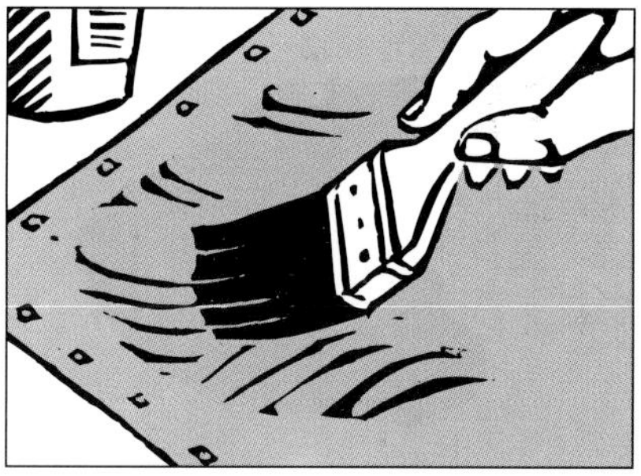

2 *Size the canvas as described, brushing on the glue and leaving it to dry, before priming it with undercoat.*

3 *Cut away any excess canvas outside the scored line on the sized, shrunk canvas, leaving a turn-under allowance.*

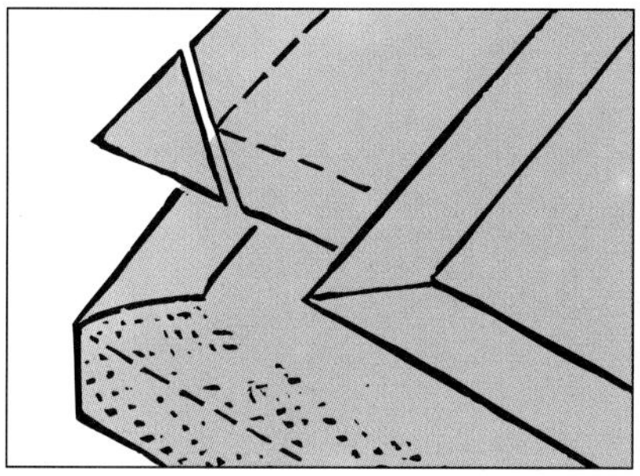

4 *Cut across the corners of the allowance diagonally; turn under the glued, trimmed edge to make a neat finish.*

Stockists and suppliers

HARD FLOORING

British Ceramic Tile Council
Federation House
Station Road
Stoke-on-Trent
Staffordshire ST4 2RT

Burlington Slate Ltd.
Cavendish House
Kirkby-in-Furness
Cumbria LA17 7UN

Elon
66 Fulham Road
London SW3 6HH

Etrusca
60 Dickson House
Ridgeway Road
Harley
Stoke-on-Trent
Staffordshire ST1 3PA

European Heritage Ltd.
56 Dawes Road
London SW6 7EJ

Fired Earth plc.
Twyford Mill
Oxford Road
Adderbury
Oxfordshire OX17 3HP

Naturestone Crossways
Silwood Road
Ascot
Berkshire SL5 0PZ

Paris Ceramics Ltd.
583 King's Road
London SW6 2EH

Stonell
Forstal House
Beltring
Kent TN17 1LY

World's End Tiles
Silverthorne Road
London SW8 3HE

FLEXIBLE FLOORING

Altro Floors
Works Road
Letchworth
Hertfordshire SG6 1NW

Carpet Tile Centre
227 Woodhouse Road
London N12 9BD

Interface Flooring Systems Ltd.
Shelf Mills
Halifax
West Yorkshire HX3 7PA

NATURAL FLOORING

The Alternative Flooring Co.
14 Anton Trading Estate
Andover
Hampshire SP10 2NJ

Crucial Trading
77 Westbourne Park Road
London W2 4BX

Three Shires Natural Flooring
3 Ptarmigan Place
Attleborough
Nuneaton
Warwickshire CB11 6RX

SOFT FLOORING

Axminster Carpets Ltd.
Gamberlake
Axminster
Devon EX1 5PQ

Brockway Carpets Ltd.
Hoobrook Works
Kidderminster
Worcestershire DY10 1XW

Christopher Farr
Handmade Rugs
115 Regents Park Road
London NW1 8UR

Stoddard Carpets Ltd.
Glenpatrick Road
Johnstone
Renfrewshire PA5 9UJ

WOOD FLOORING

The Hardwood Flooring Co. Ltd.
146/152 West End Lane
London NW6 1SD

Heritage Woodcraft
Heritage House
Hinckley Fields Industrial Estate
Leicestershire LE10 1YG

Junckers Ltd.
Wheaton Court
Commercial Centre
Wheaton Road
Essex CM8 3UJ

Milland Fine Timbers Ltd.
The Working Tree
Milland
Hampshire GU30 7JS

Tarkett
P.O. Box 173
Poyle House
Blackthorne Road
Berkshire SL3 0AZ

AUSTRALIA

Academy Tiles
20 Herbet Street
Artamon
NSW 2064

Home Hardware
414 Lower Dandenong Road
Braeside
Victoria 3195

Romano Tiles
126 Canterbury Road
Kilsyth
Victoria 3137

NEW ZEALAND

Abacus Flooring Services
375 Dominion Road
Mt Eden
Auckland

Carpet Court
Waiheke Island
145 Oceanview Road
Onroa

The Wooded Floor Co. Ltd.
74–78 Sale Street
Auckland Centre
Auckland

SOUTH AFRICA

Parker Floors
P.O. Box 1071
Jukskei Park

Tate Access Floor Systems
Pty. Ltd.
All Black Road
Boksburg North 1461
Gauteng

Tile City
31–33 Sivewright Avenue
New Doornfontein
Johannesburg

JAPAN

Loving Design Center
Shinjuku Park Tower
3-7-1, Nishi-Shinjuku
Shinjuku-ku
Tokyo 163-10

Index

Acknowledgments

1 James Mortimer/Conran Octopus; 2–3 Geoff Lung/Belle Magazine; 4 Peter Cook/View; 5 Verne; 6 *above* Ray Main; 6 *below* Sølvi Dos Santos; 7 *left* & *right* Ray Main; 8 Ken Adlard; 9 *above* Eduard Hueber (Whitney Powers); 9 *below* Antoine Rozes; 10 *above* Scott Frances/Esto; 10 *below* Andreas von Einsiedel/ Country Homes & Interiors/ Robert Harding Syndication; 11 Hotze Eisma (Karen Butler); 12 *above* Jean-Pierre Godeaut (J. Prisca); 12–13 *above* David Phelps; 12–13 *below* James Mortimer/ The Interior Archive; 13 *above right* Ingalill Snitt; 13 *below right* Fritz von der Schulenburg (Architect: Nico Rensch)/The Interior Archive; 14 John Miller; 15 Ianthe Ruthven; 16 Peter Cook (Sergison Bates); 17 Gilles de Chabaneix (Stylist: Fasoli)/Marie Claire Maison; 18 John Hall; 19 Eric Morin; 20 *above* Simon McBride; 20 *below* Rodney Hyett/ Elizabeth Whiting & Associates; 21 Richard Waite; 22 David Cripps/ Elizabeth Whiting & Associates; 24 T. Jeanson (Maison McCoy)/Stock Image Production; 25 Nina Ewald/Abode; 26 Thomas Lane; 28 Michel Claus; 29 Fritz von der Schulenburg (Dot Spikings)/The Interior Archive; 30 Scott Frances/Esto; 31 Tim Street-Porter (Designer: Barbara Barry); 32 Fritz von der Schulenburg (Architect: Nico Rensch)/The Interior Archive; 32–3 Peter Cook (Jonathon Woolf)/Hilary Coe; 33–4 Verne Fotografie; 36 Otto Baitz/Esto; 37 Michel Claus; 38 Deidi von Schaewen; 40 Hotze Eisma; 41 *above* John Heseltine; 41 *below* Christopher Simon Sykes/The Interior Archive; 42 *above* Neil Lorimer/Elizabeth Whiting & Associates; 42 *below* Nadia Mackenzie; 42–3 Paul Warchol; 43 *above* David Parmiter; 43 *below* Jean-Pierre Godeaut (Dimitri Xanthdolis); 44 *above* Mads Mogensen; 44 *below* Jean-Pierre Godeaut; 46 *left* Michael Freeman; 46 *right* Fritz von der Schulenburg/The Interior Archive; 48 Ray Main; 49 Paul Warchol; 50–1 Michel Claus; 50 *above* Georgia Glynn-Smith; 50 *below* Verne Fotografie; 51 Tim Street-Porter (Daniel Sachs); 52 Richard Felber; 54 David Phelps; 55 Ari Ashley/ Interior Archive; 56 *above* John Hall (Faulkner); 56 *below* John Hall; 58 Todd Eberle; 59 Alexander van Berge/V.T. Wonen; 60 Hotze Eisma; 60–1 John Hall; 61 *above left* Eduard Hueber (M. Burger); 61 *above right* Sinclair Till; 61 *below* Deidi von Schaewen; 62 Neil Lorimer/Elizabeth Whiting & Associates; 64 John Hall; 65 Fritz von der Schulenburg (Adelheid Gowrie)/The Interior Archive; 66 Sinclair Till; 66–7 Paul Warchol; 67 *above left* & *right* & *below* Sinclair Till; 69 Fritz von der Schulenburg (Mimmi O'Connell)/The Interior Archive; 70 James Merrell/ Woman's Journal/Robert Harding Syndication; 72 Alexander van Berge; 73 Fritz von der Schulenburg/ The World of Interiors; 74 *left* Nina Ewald/Abode; 74 *above right* Vaughan; 74 *below right* Jean-Paul Bonhommet/ Elizabeth Whiting & Associates; 75 *left* Simon Brown (John Stefanidis)/The Interior Archive; 75 Simon McBride; 76 Henry Wilson (Sophie Saren)/ The Interior Archive; 77 Ken Adlard.